Here's what readers are saying about this book...

"Easy to read and understand; hard to put down. This book saved me hours of headaches and thousands of dollars."
Jo Ann Harris – Sacramento, California

"The writing style is clear and concise. It's straight to the point and factual, yet with a healthy dose of entertainment and humor, which makes the book fun, easy to read, and captivating. It's a real matter-of-fact, hands-on guide from and for the everyday life of a small factor."
Ralf Bieler – Tequesta, Florida

"Factoring Case Studies has already saved me at least $1500. That was the 'initial investment' in a little business deal I was just presented with that I would have considered not long ago. But after reading this book I kept seeing the letter R in a triangle (the book's icon for 'Risk'). I saw very few of the positive symbols as he spoke. I quickly dismissed his proposition."
Michael J. Minicucci – New Hope, Minnesota

"An eye-opening account. Excellent value for the price."
J.M. – College Station, Texas

"Reading this book is like sitting down with a small group of practicing small factors and having each one tell you about some of their deals. This book is an incredible value considering the time and money it will save most people who will read and learn from it. I can think of no other place where this kind of real world information would be available."
Michael C. Minchew – Ideal, Georgia

"Simple and clear. I am requiring all of my staff to read this book along with the other books in the series."
Ken Earnhardt – Mt. Pleasant, South Carolina

"This is not a book. It is a survival manual for factors. I am going to keep a copy on my desk at all times."
Reed Sawyer – *American Cash Flow Journal*®

"Straightforward and easy to follow, this book gives a 'college degree in real world situations' and what can, should or would be done by both honest and dishonest people."
Ed Naglich – Etters, Pennsylvania

"This is one of the best ways of learning about small receivables factoring. Learning by example without experiencing the unfortunate losses is worth its weight in successful transactions. It should be required reading for folks new to the business. The writing style is very easy to read. I loved the name changes."
J.G. – New York, New York

"This book is an 'easy read' because of its short case studies and the brief analysis following each story. You can stop at the end of any case study and pick up the book again later without losing continuity. Each case study helps the reader understand the many subtleties that either makes a factoring transaction go well or turn sour."
Virginia Sternberg – Mill Creek, Washington

"The writing style is readable and easy to understand. The book's value lies in the ultimate many hundreds – or even thousands – of dollars that can be saved by learning from others' mistakes."
Kelley R.J. Tetzlaff – Tempe, Arizona

"Factual, objective and compassionate, good-natured, humorous wisdom. I found the client and company names to be illustrative and witty descriptions for the characters. The writing style is conversational and approachable. Well worth the investment!"
Joseph Leight – Santa Cruz, California

"I enjoy Jeff Callender's writing style. Reading his books on factoring is like having on your team, and having a conversation with, a very well-informed and capable coach-player. I found the information on the marketing methods to be very valuable."
Rob Columbus – Santa Fe, New Mexico

Factoring Case Studies

Learn and Profit from
Experienced Small Factors

Jeff Callender

DASH POINT PUBLISHING

Federal Way, Washington

Factoring Case Studies
Learn and Profit from Experienced Small Factors

by Jeff Callender

Published by:
Dash Point Publishing, Inc.
P.O. Box 25591
Federal Way, WA 98093-2591 U.S.A.

Web Sites:	www.DashPointPublishing.com
	www.DashPointFinancial.com
	www.SmallFactor.com
	www.Factor-Tips.com
Email:	info@DashPointPublishing.com

©2003, 2005 by Jeff Callender

ISBN, print edition	0-9709365-7-5
ISBN, eBook edition	0-9709365-8-3

Names of people and companies who are described as clients or customers of the small factors in this book have been intentionally changed. Any similarity between these names and names of actual people and companies is unintended and purely coincidental.

While every reasonable attempt has been made to obtain accurate information, the author and publisher hereby disclaim any liability for problems due to errors, omissions, or changed information in this publication.

Printed in the United States of America.

Library of Congress Control Number 2002096352

Dedication

To the Small Factors
Who Contributed to This Book

Also by Jeff Callender

Books and eBooks

The Small Factor Series includes:

1. ***Factoring Fundamentals***
   How You Can Make Large Returns in Small Receivables
   ©2003, 2005

2. ***Factoring Small Receivables***
   How to Make Money in Little Deals the Big Guys Brush Off
   ©1995, 1996, 1998, 2001, 2002, 2003, 2005 (7th edition)

3. ***Factoring Case Studies***
   Learn and Profit from Experienced Small Factors
   ©2003, 2005

4. ***Unlocking the Cash in Your Company***
   How to Get Unlimited Funds without a Loan
   ©2003, 2005

Marketing Tools for Small Factors and Consultants
A Hands-On Guide to Methods that Work ©2004

Factoring Wisdom
Short Sayings and Straight Talk for New & Small Factors
©2004, 2005

Unlocking the Cash in Your Cleaning Company
By Jeff Callender and Vincent Tillis. ©2004

Growing Your Company without Debt*:*
How Today's Small Business Can Get Cash by Tomorrow
(Booklet, eBooklet, & Audio)   ©1996, 1998, 2002

Software/Forms

Record Keeping Templates   ©2002
APR and Income Calculators   ©2002
Factoring Consultation Form   ©2003

Internet Resources

www.DashPointPublishing.com Web Site
www.Factor-Tips.com (free ezine for factors)
www.SmallFactor.com Web Site
www.DashPointFinancial.com Web Site
www.BluBeagle.com Web Site

Contents

About the Author

Jeff Callender grew up in Riverside, California, and graduated from Whittier College near Los Angeles. He received his Master of Divinity from Pacific School of Religion in Berkeley, California, in 1978. He then served as a Presbyterian pastor in three congregations in Washington state until 1993.

Jeff has been involved in factoring since 1994. At that time he became a Certified Factoring Specialist through the International Factoring Institute of Orlando, Florida. He then started his company (now Dash Point Financial Services, Inc.) and soon began factoring small receivables.

He writes a monthly column on small receivables for *The American Cash Flow Journal®,* a national publication of the American Cash Flow Association, and is a regular speaker at the ACFA's annual Cash Flow conventions. He funds a portfolio factoring clients and provides numerous resources and consulting services for people interested in becoming small factors. For more information, go to his web sites at www.SmallFactor.com, www.Factor-Tips.com, and www.DashPointFinancial.com. To order his resource materials, go to www.DashPointPublishing.com.

Jeff is married and the father of a grown son and daughter.

Acknowledgments

I would like to thank the following people for the important parts they played in creating this book:

The **contributing writers** who generously gave their time, experiences, wisdom, and insights. Without them this book could not have been written.

Richard Shapiro for his inspirational creativity.

Jo Callender for her proofreading and editing skills, as well as a number of others who previewed the book and made many helpful suggestions.

Cover design by Christine Salo of Hunter's Moon Graphics. Email HuntrsMoon@aol.com

Cover picture by EyeWire Collection/Getty Images

Important Notice

Preface

This is the third book in **The Small Factor Series,** which opens the door to the remarkable and lucrative investment of factoring small business receivables. While you don't need to read the other books to understand this one, the purpose of **Factoring Case Studies***: Learn and Profit from Experienced Small Factors* is to educate and illustrate the many principles and instructions given in the other books.

The first title, **Factoring Fundamentals***: How You Can Make Large Returns in Small Receivables,* introduces the reader to the basic concepts of factoring. *Fundamentals* describes what factoring is, how it works, businesses which can benefit, the remarkable returns possible, risks involved, and how to minimize those risks. It helps the reader define the meaning of "success," whether factoring is an appropriate move for his or her circumstances, and closes with a look at four small factors who enter the field from very diverse backgrounds, with quite different purposes.

The second book, **Factoring Small Receivables***: How to Make Money in Little Deals the Big Guys Brush Off,* is the "nuts and bolts" hands-on manual for running a small factoring operation. It includes first-hand lessons from the factoring industry, identifies where to find operating capital, provides marketing strategies, and describes numerous common mistakes small factors all too often make. There are discussions on due diligence, credit reports, reviews of factoring software, a chapter on record keeping, a sample factoring transaction from start to finish with an accompanying flowchart, and a multitude of online and offline resources available for small factors.

The fourth book, **Unlocking the Cash in Your Company***: How to Get Unlimited Funds without a Loan,* is written for potential factoring clients – owners of small businesses who can utilize factoring to benefit their business. This book compares factoring to more traditional financing, explains who is eligible, suggests features and services to look for in a factor, and discusses how to find a factor. *Unlocking the Cash* also describes the application process, due diligence procedures to expect, what to tell customers, normal factoring procedures, and faulty assumptions people often make about factoring. It concludes by encouraging the reader to visualize specific enhancements and advantages factoring can provide his or her business.

While **Unlocking the Cash** is primarily written for prospective clients, its point of view provides further insight for those who wish to participate as small factors. The book also serves as a marketing tool to prospective clients from factors and brokers seeking new business.

The present book, **Factoring Case Studies**, stands on its own and can be read apart from the others. Yet *Case Studies* provides those who have read the other books a large corner piece of the jigsaw of the factoring experience. This book gives flesh and blood to the crucial yet academic information imparted in the other volumes.

One can read the other books without this one and still become a successful small factor. However, this book describes in numerous, unique, and very personal ways what you're in for as a factor of small business receivables. Some of these stories will encourage – maybe even compel you – to enter the arena. Others might well scare you away. In either case, you'll find these case studies educational, revealing, thought-provoking, and even entertaining.

Jeff Callender

Part 1

Setting the Stage

Introduction

What This Book Is About

In the first two books of *The Small Factor Series,* I included examples from my own factoring business to illustrate several points. Readers of those books may remember my very first client, the carpet cleaner whose receivables were literally piled in shoe boxes when we started. Organization was not his middle name, and unknown to both of us he factored several invoices that had already been paid when we began. Thus began my education as a small factor.

You may also recall another client, a PhD in the medical field who lived in my neighborhood, whose child my daughter baby-sat. That client received her first advance factoring one invoice, then skipped town after "copping" the payment check. I still shake my head over that one.

The purpose of these and other stories was to give real-life, human examples in what was heavily information-laden material. While small factors definitely need the information to earn the remarkably high returns within their reach, they also need to realize how very human the experience of factoring is.

This is a very people-centric enterprise. If individuals don't fascinate you, you probably will not find factoring very interesting. Exasperating at times – yes; quite lucrative at times – no question; but *interesting*…no. The purpose of this book is not only to illustrate and educate, but to share the fascination I find in factoring.

If you don't understand what people are really like deep down, the heavy dose of human nature you'll receive from factoring will be quite an eye-opener. I have found when you deal with people's money, you are handling something that over time reveals their inner nature. You will sometimes be surprised with what you find, as their outer facade is peeled away and the inner nature revealed.

Sometimes those surprises are pleasant and you find a true heart of gold; such moments and such souls are an honor to behold. Other times you expose a heart that is twisted and wretched, and you regret having been part of its unmasking. You also regret the loss of money, time, and the stress you experienced because of this person.

Peeling back that outer skin and revealing the inner nature is what this book is about. It's far more than just a book on alternative financing, though it is that as well.

How This Book Came to Be

One day I was speaking with a colleague (one of this book's contributors, actually) who was having a seemingly never-ending saga with a very trying client. As the story unfolded into yet another unbelievable episode, I found myself thinking, "What an experience! The stories from this client alone could teach loads about the business of factoring small receivables. What would result if I could put together a collection of several true stories like this?!"

As that thought germinated I came to see that an album of stories from this colleague and several others would have great educational value. A group of stories – factoring case studies – would not only illustrate in human terms the principles, instructions, warnings, and suggestions made in the first two books; it would be both fascinating and entertaining. Thus this book took its embryonic form.

I put together some thoughts as to what these case studies might include, and assembled a list of small factors I knew with various levels of factoring experience. I contacted these people and asked if they would be willing to share their experiences with one to four clients for a new book. The response was strong and their replies make up the pages that follow.

Each contributor was given the same instructions for creating the case studies. In short, I asked for "the good, the bad, and the ugly" of their factoring experiences. As you will see, each writes with his or her own style and outlook. Below are the guidelines each contributor was given as he or she sat down to write.

"For each case study, describe:
- How you and the client found each other.
- The industry the client is in, the client's product or service, and to whom the client sells.
- Why he/she wanted to factor, and why he/she wanted to factor with you.
- The approximate factoring volume.
- How you structured your rates, advances and rebates.
- Why this particular client stands out from others.

For the 'good' clients describe:
- What specifically made this a valuable client to you.
- How long he/she factored with you.
- What appealed to you when you accepted this client.
- What did/do you like about the client as he/she continue/d to factor.
- What features in him/her you look for in new prospects.
- If you were just starting to factor again, what you would do the same, and what you would do differently.

For the clients that were 'bad' experiences, describe:
- The chronology of when and how things went south.
- Whether the problems were of the client's making and/or a result of your mistakes.
- What specific mistakes you made that you would do differently next time.
- Whether the client tried to defraud you, either intentionally or unintentionally, and if so how.
- Whether the root of the problem was client mismanagement, incompetence, and/or personal problems/circumstances such as illness or divorce, etc.
- How your experience with this client has affected your procedures, general practices, or industries/clients/debtors you no longer accept."

Not one of these case studies is made up. Every story is true and each client is real. For the sake of anonymity, company names and personal names have obviously been changed. The names given them are monikers or acronyms which describe the essence of each business or experience in a few words. Hopefully they will bring you a smile or two, if not a good laugh.

With these preliminaries in place, let's look at an overview to help you understand the book's layout, the icons in the margins and their meaning, and the analyses that follow.

Overview

The Contributors

All eight contributors to these case studies are honest-to-goodness, bona-fide small factors across the country. Their names are real and their companies are very much in business. Many received training as factoring brokers and later started buying receivables as funding sources. Others began factoring without any training and learned the business on their own.

The contributors have quite diverse backgrounds. All are Americans living in the USA and one is a naturalized citizen from Lebanon. Their formal educations range from high school graduates to college graduates to an MBA to a PhD in electrical engineering. Their experiences prior to entering factoring include working as a handyman, an industrial engineer, a bookkeeper and office clerk, a national phone company employee, an electrician, a banker, an owner of a textile recycling company, a university professor, a secretary and stay-at-home mom, and an operations manager for a local phone company.

Of the eight small factoring companies represented, three are family-run in which both the husband and wife work the business. Of the five non-family operations, two have business partners, two are one-person operations, and three factor full-time. Six are home-based businesses and two work from an outside office. Their homes stretch from coast to coast and include Oregon, California, Nevada, Arizona, Illinois, Michigan, Maryland, and South Carolina.

One writer was a business owner who factored his receivables. That person began as a factor in the early 1980's, while the others started in the 1990's. Three currently focus more on brokering deals than funding. The others spend most of their time funding transactions, and broker occasional deals as they deem appropriate.

The Case Studies

There are twenty-one case studies written by the eight small factors. Ten of these studies could be considered good experiences, while eleven are negative (…and a few of those downright awful). I want to point out this percentage of bad experiences does not reflect the proportion of good/bad clients in the portfolios of most factors. If it did, there would be very few factors in business! Most factors have a negative experience from time to time, but the vast majority of their clients and transactions hum along at a relatively smooth and steady pace. Make no mistake, however: the unpleasant ones are hard to forget! As you read, notice how many negative case studies occur when the factor is new to the business.

The disproportionately high number of "lemons" is included here for instructional purposes. While you learn a great deal from good client experiences, you also learn plenty from the bad. That's why the negative case studies are in this book in such abundance. Their number is not intended to scare you away from factoring, but is included to give you several first-hand accounts of the troubling situations that can arise – and give you some handles as to how to steer clear.

Marketing is always a key issue for people starting business. To help with this matter, I've summarized below the client industries that are included in these case studies, as well as the marketing methods or referral sources the factors used to obtain these clients.

Client Industries
Advertising Agency
Carpet Cleaner
Commercial Cleaners
Construction Supplier
Floor Surface Preparer
Food Processor
Garment Distributor
Importer
Internet Service Provider (2)

Landscaper
Manufacturer
Map Maker
Printer
Screen Printer
Security Guard Service
Temporary Agencies for:
   Office Workers
   Home Health Care Nurses
   Nurses in Retirement Homes
   Traveling Nurses
Tool and Die Shop

<u>Marketing Methods/Referral Sources</u>
Attorney
Banker
Bookkeeper
Factoring Broker (2)
Financial Services Account Manager
Friend/Acquaintance (2)
Internet Matchmaking Site
Networking Group/Meeting (5)
Other Factor (2)
Other Factoring Client (3)
Other Factoring Client's Customer
Public Speaking
Relative
SCORE (Service Corps of Retired Executives)

Chapters Structure

Part 2 contains all twenty-one case studies. Each small factor provides from one to four case studies, and each writer's contribution makes up a separate chapter. The beginning of each writer's section provides contact information, a brief biographical sketch of the factor, his or her background prior to factoring, and a short description of his or her business currently.

The case studies follow the writers' introductions. The words are their own. I have provided some editorial touches for clarity and added icons in the margins as running commentary. I have also changed the clients' company and owner names (except for the chapter by Richard Shapiro, whose revised names were already perfect), added occasional footnotes, and provided a closing analysis of each case study. Thus this book is a shared effort between the contributors and myself.

Icon Explanations

Most pages have icons in the left margin which point out positive or negative information described. Triangles and red flags are negative, while the others are positive. Below is a brief explanation and the ideas each icon conveys. On the next page a bookmark is provided to tear out and use for easy reference to these icons.

Positive Icons

 Benefit of Factoring – A benefit factoring provides the client is conveyed. Use these in your marketing!

 Desirable Client Feature – A desirable aspect of a client is expressed. The more of these you find in a prospect, the better.

 Due Diligence – A standard due diligence activity is described.

 Common Factoring Practice – A normal factoring procedure is being followed.

 Risk Minimizer – This is a precaution or action which lessens the factor's risk. Learn to weave these into your own practices.

 Good Advice – So pay attention!

Common Sense – One of the most vital assets of any factor.

 Mark of Success – Experiences which make factoring so gratifying for everyone involved.

Negative Icons

 Risk – The factor is taking a chance or the client is acting in a way which increases the factor's risk.

 Mistake – A mistake is being made by the factor or client.

If the error is the factor's, he/she is making one of many "Common Mistakes" listed in *Factoring Small Receivables* or is doing something he/she may regret later.

If the error is the client's, he/she is making a management decision (often without realizing it) that may prove costly to both the client and factor.

 Over-concentration – The factor has too much money concentrated in this particular client, customer, or invoice. This can pose a grave danger to the survival of the factor's business.

 Fraud – The client has committed a fraudulent act. Very, very bad.

 Red Flag – When these come up…watch out!

Factoring Case Studies
by Jeff Callender

<u>Icon Reference</u>

Benefit of
Factoring

Desirable
Client Feature

Common
Factoring Practice

Due
Diligence

Good
Advice

Common
Sense

Risk
Minimizer

Mark of
Succes

Risk

Mistake

Over
Concentration

Fraud

Red Flag

Part 2

Case Studies

Premier Funding

Contact Information
Premier Funding
Kari and Kevin Clark
Lebanon, OR
Email: premierfunding@juno.com

Kari and Kevin Clark

Kevin entered the Coast Guard following high school where he did communications systems installation. Following his tour of service he worked for an independent phone company as a service technician. He soon became an operations manager and worked in the industry for 16 years. He is now working the factoring business full time with Kari from their home.

Kari attended community college and later worked as a secretary in the insurance industry until her children were born, and was a stay-at-home mom until 1996. At that time the Clarks built and financed their home using only credit cards and a line of credit, which introduced them to the idea of creative financing.

Shortly thereafter they attended the Diversified Cash Flow Institute and started their business as note and factoring brokers. In their first year of business they made the Million Dollar Club of the American Cash Flow Association from some very large transactions. They bought their first factoring client's receivables in 1998, whose case study follows. In addition to factoring small receivables, they also broker purchase order funding, large commercial loans, equipment leasing, and asset-based loans.

Since beginning the business they have been involved in the local Chamber of Commerce and the Portland Chapter of the American Cash Flow Association. They have also participated in the American Business Connection, a local business networking group.

The Clarks volunteer time for the Trauma Intervention Program, an organization that works with fire departments, police departments and emergency agencies to provide emotional first aid to traumatized citizens immediately following a tragic event. They are the parents of five sons and teach parenting classes at their church. Kari volunteers once a week in the office of their children's school, and also is a substitute teacher there. The Clarks enjoy traveling, snow skiing, and spend a lot of time at soccer, baseball, and basketball games, and other programs in which their kids are involved.

1

Freddy Reddy's Steady Carpet Cleaning

While attending a business leads group meeting one April, I gave a brief presentation about my business, including factoring. After the meeting, Fred Reddy, the owner of a commercial carpet cleaning business named Freddy Reddy's Steady Carpet Cleaning, approached me about helping him with his cash flow needs.

Fred explained that he had been in business for over twenty years but was terrible at bookkeeping and was sure he was losing money on invoices he couldn't track. His business was barely surviving, despite the fact that he catered to some large property management companies. I explained in further detail the factoring process.

Kevin and I had already come up with an advance rate and discount structure based on what other factors were doing. Fred had never even heard of factoring before hearing me speak, but realizing how it could benefit his business, he wanted to get started with the paperwork immediately.

I used a simple application and charged him $100 for running the D&B and credit reports. Fred wanted to personally contact each of the clients he wanted to factor. I made up labels for him to use on his invoices, notifying his clients to make checks payable to his company and send them to my mailing address.

I purchased a Special Power of Attorney form from a local stationery store and used another person in our leads group to notarize it and all our factoring agreements. I then went to my bank and explained what I was going to be doing and gave them a copy of the Special Power of Attorney.

DD

We set up QuickBooks Pro on our computer and took hours figuring out how to enter the invoices, advance amounts, and rebates. Once our UCC lien was filed, all the paperwork was in and recorded, and our accounting system was set up, we were ready to go.

✓

Premier Funding advances 70% of the invoice amount. We charge 4% for the first 30 days and 2% additional each 15 days thereafter, up to 12% for 75 to 90 days. At 90 days, we perform modified recourse; that is, we exchange an invoice that is unpaid after 90 days for a new invoice. Sometimes we take the recourse amount out of a rebate we would otherwise give Fred.

DD

✓

For example, let's say we advanced Fred 70% on a $100 invoice 90 days ago. Fred owes us $70 for the amount we advanced, plus 12%, or $12, for our discount for a total chargeback of $82. If we are getting ready to advance on another batch of invoices, we withhold the chargeback amount from the check. If we don't have an advance to give him, we subtract the chargeback amount from the next rebate. This has worked out well for us, since we keep a close eye on Fred's A/R aging report. We send Fred a copy of his A/R aging report with each advance and/or rebate check, which is almost every week.

✓

We provided Fred with a Schedule of Accounts form to submit with each batch of invoices. It was clear from the first set of invoices and account schedules that we were going to have to refine our process for purchasing invoices. Fred's invoices were very small, averaging $57 each, with the first batch totaling $2,387. It took Kevin and me about two hours to enter bills (the actual invoice amount), enter invoices (so we would be able to receive payments for the bills), and finally pay bills (the advance amount). Yes, it was a three-step process to make the advance. We did not use any factoring database software. We entered the address of each job location for each invoice.

Fred used handwritten invoices with a very unusual invoice numbering system. Instead of an invoice with a number like 2301, it would be 01-21-04A. This made perfect sense to him, but for our accounting it was a nightmare. The first two sets of digits stood for the month and date the work was performed. The last set indicated the number of jobs for that date and customer. In the above example, it would be January 21, the fourth job of the day and the A stood for the first job of the day for a particular customer.

Since Fred's largest customers are property management companies, it was common to have several jobs for a particular customer at the same property on one day. The other huge problem we faced was that Fred had more than one truck, resulting in numerous invoices with duplicate invoice numbers.

On several occasions during that first year of factoring, Fred mentioned how much one particular customer enjoyed working with me. Knowing how this customer felt I took the liberty to call the bookkeeper to discuss Fred's invoice numbering system. We agreed it would simplify the bookkeeping for everyone doing business with Fred, including Fred's staff, to use invoices with pre-printed invoice numbers. One year after Fred began factoring, he switched over to the new invoices which meant I no longer had to enter all those addresses, since duplicate invoice numbers would cease being an issue.

Fred has been factoring now for over four years. His business has continued to grow, almost to the point he doesn't need our services anymore. However, for larger customers who normally don't pay until the 30 to 60 day range, he still prefers to factor them.

Fred started off factoring a monthly average volume of $3,290 his first year. His second, third, and fourth year he averaged $6,748, $6,450, and $5,077 respectively per month. He only factors three customers now, but early on the number he factored was about ten. Fred takes advantage of large volume and cash discounts from his vendors with his improved cash flow from factoring.

I have simplified my processing so much that it now takes me less than 30 minutes, start to finish, to do an advance.

Because of Fred's small invoices and low monthly volume, he has been the perfect first client. We have enjoyed watching his business flourish. He enjoys getting his advances and rebates quickly from us. Fred continues to submit invoices every other week or two. By running credit checks prior to funding his new customers, we have been able to caution him about a couple of them, probably avoiding some non-pays. Fred has given us several leads for new factoring clients, which we have been able to broker to other factors. In fact, one client he referred has been factoring for over four years, during which time we have received steady broker commissions.

There are several things that appealed to me about factoring Fred when he approached me. He had a very good reputation with the people in the leads group I belonged to. He had been in business for over 20 years in the same small community. When Fred gets excited about something, he does not hesitate to share with others. I knew if I ran my factoring business professionally and helped Fred pull out of his financial problems, he would in turn bring me business. I look for similar features in new prospects.

If we were just starting to factor again, we would try to find additional money at a lower cost. We were too generous with one investor and our process was too complicated with another.

The first investor loaned us $4,000. We paid him 2% per month on the whole $4,000, which we felt was too much considering he was getting paid even if less than $4,000 was out on invoices. The second investor started off by paying us the amount of each advance. We would pay him 1% per month on the actual amount outstanding.

This became too complicated because Fred would factor more invoices before we had received all the money due on previous advances. This caused us to advance Fred the money we were going to send back to our investor. Both investors were happy with their ends of the deals.

We are thankful that we have been able to continue to factor Fred ourselves during his largest volume of factoring. For most of our four and a half years of factoring Fred, we have used our own money from either credit cards or a home equity line of credit.

+   +   +

Analysis

The Clarks started factoring in much the same way as many small factors: part-time with one very small client. Because he was unfamiliar with factoring and Kevin and Kari were new funders, both learned the process together. Fortunately Fred's volume was quite small and the funds put at risk by the Clarks were relatively low, at least by ordinary factoring standards. Both learned together and both businesses have prospered from the relationship. In turn, taking excellent care of Fred has resulted in new business the Clarks have been able to broker, instilled a great deal of good will, and helped create a good reputation for them in their community. Fred's enthusiasm and desire to tell others about Premier Funding is the most effective and least expensive marketing any factor can use.

Fred fits many characteristics of an excellent client, especially for small factors just starting out. He is honest, and has been in business long enough to have earned a good reputation as a business owner and a prominent place in his networking group. What's more, he instantly recognized the value of factoring and saw how it would not only improve his company's cash flow, but with the Clarks' help, improve his ragged billing procedures.

The Clarks have been wise (and fortunate) to begin factoring with a client like Fred. They also provide an excellent model, combining their previous and ongoing cash flow brokering business with slowly becoming a funding source. Gaining a taste for the high returns factoring provides, they have not over-reacted and attempted to take on more new clients than they can manage or afford. They are content having the one excellent client in Fred, which shows wisdom and an understanding of their capabilities.

Kari and Kevin have also shown a judicious use of their factoring capital. Using other people's money, they learned from trial and error two ways *not* to obtain money. They paid too much (24% APR) in the first case, and set up administrative complications in the second. They have used credit cards and a home equity line of credit to replace the earlier borrowed funds; while this is not a good idea for most people, the Clarks have made it work. This is in part because Fred was already a tried and tested client before they began using these funds, and because his cash needs were modest. If Fred had proven to be dishonest and the Clarks had taken a loss, their own credit could have been jeopardized. Further, if the Clarks were to take on several new clients and had more serious capital needs to fund them, credit cards and putting one's home at risk are not good ideas, despite their easy accessibility.

Kevin and Kari also cleverly came up with a way to use QuickBooks to track their factoring records. While this program is not written for factoring and cannot provide sophisticated database management that factoring software provides, they were able to figure out a way to make it work for their relatively simple needs...and saved a bundle of money in the process. However, should they want to take on numerous clients and use the services of brokers to gain new business, they will need to look beyond QuickBooks to fill their needs.

Premier Funding is providing exceptional value to their client.

- Their dependable cash advances and prompt rebates enable Fred to take advantage of volume and cash discounts.

- They have improved and streamlined his billing system, such that even his customers appreciate the difference and are no doubt more inclined to continue doing business with him.

- They provide credit screening services which have saved Fred money and headaches by avoiding potential deadbeat customers.

No wonder Fred likes to tell everyone he meets about how Premier Funding has helped his business!

Mach 1 Funding

Contact Information
Mach 1 Funding, Inc.
Mike Abed, President
800 La Terraza Blvd., Suite 230
Escondido, CA 92025-3898
Tel.:   (760) 480-8000
Fax: (760) 745-2233
E-mail: Mike@mach1funding.com
Web site: www.mach1funding.com

Dr. Hikmat (Mike) A. Abed

A graduate of the University of California at Berkeley with a Ph.D. in Electrical Engineering, Dr. Hikmat (Mike) Abed's background includes more than twenty years of business experience in senior executive positions and several years of teaching graduate and undergraduate courses in Engineering, Mathematics and Physics. He published four books and several research papers in those fields. He has also participated in and conducted numerous seminars and training programs in business administration, management development, technical training and power utilities operations.

Mike is a Certified Factoring Specialist (CFS), a Certified Capital Specialist (CCS), a Million Dollar Club member, a Master Broker of the American Cash Flow Association (ACFA), and the recipient of the American Cash Flow Corporation's (ACFC) 2002 President's Award. He is

Charter President and founding member of the San Diego Cash Flow Association (SDCFA).

Mike has published several articles on business funding in trade and business journals, presented several business funding seminars to business clubs and professional associations, and has been university guest lecturer on business funding on a regular basis.

He is the founder and president of Mach 1 Funding, which specializes in helping small and medium size businesses with their cash flow by providing them with immediate cash. Mach 1 Funding is a funding source for factoring and purchase order funding and is a master broker for all other financial transactions. Mike is involved in his factoring business full-time.

2

Rock Solid Security Services

Rock Solid Security Services is a husband and wife company providing security guards to their customers, which include residential and commercial compounds, apartment complexes, construction sites, etc.

Rock Solid was referred to me by a relative of mine. Jeeves and Holly Goodfellow wanted their company to grow, but did not have the capital for such growth. We signed them on in October. In about two and a half months we funded 37 invoices totaling about $60,000. Almost immediately, Rock Solid started experiencing growth with their newly found working capital. They were ecstatic and wrote us a resounding testimonial.

The account was running like clockwork. The great majority of invoices paid within 30 days. Only very few went to 31-60 days, but none ever exceeded 60 days, because if any invoice gets to that point, Rock Solid would buy it back.

After a few months of factoring, Rock Solid started picking bigger customers in addition to acquiring most of the customers of a competitor who went out of business. A major issue surfaced. Jeeves and Holly came to us and said that some of their largest customers were adamant about refusing to deal with factors. This put them in a dilemma because they wanted to keep those customers, but they could not service their accounts without factoring.

Mach 1 Funding, being a factor that prides itself on its caring for its customers, its positioning as a problem solver rather than a service salesman, its creativity and its flexibility, suggested the following solution.

Because of the extra risk undertaken by Mach 1 Funding by not verifying the invoices for such customers, we requested Rock Solid to:

1. Change their mailing address to our address so that the checks (in their names) will be mailed to our address.

2. Sign a personal guarantee, which we normally do not ask from our clients

3. Keep an amount equal to 10% of their estimated monthly factoring volume in their reserve account over and above their normal accrued reserve.

Jeeves and Holly gladly accepted. We did the necessary paperwork and started factoring the new customers. Additionally, because of Rock Solid's need for more cash due to its accelerated growth, they started submitting all their invoices, even the smaller ones, which we accepted to accommodate their needs.

In less than a month, their factoring volume more than doubled from an average of $20,000 to $30,000, to $70,000 to $80,000 per month. Yet the account remained in top shape maintaining its clockwork performance without a hitch. Not a single invoice remained outstanding beyond 60 days, though the overwhelming majority paid within 30 days. The fact that Rock Solid bills its customers on a biweekly basis, rather than a monthly basis, has helped.

In the nine months we have had this account with a spotless record, we have funded 344 invoices totaling $404,000 with an average earned discount of 7%.

Although the hardest and costliest lessons are learned from bad experiences, we learned very valuable free lessons from this good account:

1. Take calculated risks when your gut feeling tolerates it, because the rewards might be worth it.

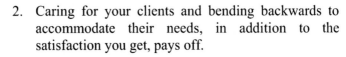

2. Caring for your clients and bending backwards to accommodate their needs, in addition to the satisfaction you get, pays off.

3. Creativity and flexibility have their rewards.

The assumption that one $10,000 invoice is better than ten $1,000 invoices is not necessarily true. We found, in general, that collecting small invoices is much easier than collecting bigger invoices. Smaller invoices pay faster than bigger invoices. As such the risk in factoring smaller invoices is much less than in factoring bigger invoices, although the administrative work is much more.

A slow paying account is not a better income generator than a fast paying account. I would take an account that pays within 30 days anytime over an account that pays within 90 days, not only because of peace of mind, but also because of higher returns.

+   +   +

Analysis

This is the type of client every factor desires. Security guard services and temp agencies are often excellent factoring clients (though not always, as we'll see later) because

1) They absolutely must meet payroll to stay in business.

2) They wait too long for customer payments to arrive in order to meet payroll.

3) They usually grow quickly when factoring provides the cash they so badly need.

Look at Rock Solid's growth in monthly factoring volume: sales roughly tripled in just the first two months! Cash is king, especially in the temp staffing and security guard world. The only caveat here is to be sure such a client can manage his/her growth, especially such rapid growth.

Another highly desirable feature of this case study: most of Rock Solid's accounts pay in 30 days or less, with very few going as long as 60. As Mike so wisely points out, he prefers to "take an account that pays within 30 days anytime over an account that pays within 90 days." Heed his advice! Your risk is less and your return is higher because your money turns more often. And yes, you do sleep better.

Mike also sagely notes that small invoices tend to pay more quickly than larger ones. When a customer has a long list of bills to pay, little ones are often dealt with faster to "get them out of the way." This is frequent thinking in many bookkeepers' and business owners' minds and can work in the small factor's favor.

Finally, this case study shows the benefit of excellent customer service. Compared to factoring rates and advances, good service is less often discussed; but service is one of the most important features of the business. As we'll see in other case studies, dissatisfied clients seek a different factor not just to find better rates: they look elsewhere because the factor they have is inflexible, uncaring, or just provides lousy customer service. Mike's personal care for his client in this case study illustrates a big reason why his factoring business does so well. He cares about his clients and goes to great lengths to meet their needs.

3

We Always eXpect More Floors

David D. Shiner, owner of We Always eXpect More (WAXM) Floors, a company specializing in preparation of surfaces for flooring, was introduced to me by a CPA.

Having had bad experiences with his ex-partner that left him in financial ruin, David decided to start his own business, WAXM. His CPA introduced him to me as his client and friend. David had heavy debt to his ex-partner with quite unfavorable terms on his equipment. Further, he was saddled with an IRS lien that required monthly installment payments.

I met with David in the office of the CPA and I found him an energetic young man with a very likable character and the potential for a promising future. I decided to accept him as a factoring client and started factoring his small invoices, which ranged between $1,000 and $3,000 in January his first year.

He had a sizable profit margin in these small jobs. He started growing very fast and his invoices started getting bigger and bigger. David was ecstatic and wrote me a very powerful testimonial. He had plans to grow to $500,000 by the first year and to $1 million by his second year in business.

By the end of his first year in business, we had already factored about $500,000 in invoices. The transactions were going like clock work to the point that I considered WAXM an exemplary client. As such, and since his factoring volume was growing steadily, I lowered his discount discount 3 times and raised his advance rate once. We started with a discount of 6% for 30 days and an advance of 60%. Within

15 months the discount was 4.5% and the advance rate 70%. In effect, this was an overall reduction in his factoring discounts of about 36%.

Looking through the rear view mirror, I can now say that trouble started at the beginning of the second year of business (and factoring) of WAXM.

Encouraged by his growth and exuberant about his increased cash flow, David wanted to grow at a faster pace. He commissioned one of his long-time friends, Bob Olbuddy, to acquire new jobs for him for a percentage of the contract value of each job. Bob would earn 18% of every payment received by David from such jobs.

When I learned about that arrangement, I immediately detected trouble and warned David about it. The way he looked at it, his profit margin was 30%. If he gave Bob 18%, he would still be left with 12 % – icing on the cake to his way of thinking; money which he would not have received otherwise.

There were 3 flaws to this thinking:

1. With the bigger jobs he was obtaining, David would not maintain his 30% margin. It had to drop down considerably to be competitive.

2. Payments on such jobs were slower, making the factoring cost higher.

3. David was using the bulk of his resources to do those bigger jobs with the substantially lower margins, while doing fewer smaller jobs with the higher margins.

By the time David realized his flawed strategy six months later, he was already in financial trouble. He parted ways with Bob Olbuddy and hired an in-house marketing person, Marcus Dolittle. Five months later, and $20,000 poorer with no marketing results from Marcus, David realized his second major mistake and fired Dolittle.

In the meantime, upon lowering my discount another 10%, David brought me a batch of invoices totaling more than $150,000. He wanted to take advantage of the reduced

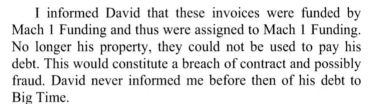

discounts, pay off what I was owed on some outstanding factored invoices, and obtain cash for the balance of the advance. Out of this batch there were two invoices totaling $104,000 for a single customer, Big Time Contractors.

I verified the new invoices and received acknowledgement of their approval from the customer and advanced funds. A few months later, when these invoices still had not been paid and with consistent follow-up, David admitted that Big Time would not pay me because these factored invoices were used to offset other obligations David owed Big Time. Committing fraud in this way was David's third major mistake.

I informed David that these invoices were funded by Mach 1 Funding and thus were assigned to Mach 1 Funding. No longer his property, they could not be used to pay his debt. This would constitute a breach of contract and possibly fraud. David never informed me before then of his debt to Big Time.

David acknowledged the predicament but pleaded fervently not to pursue this issue with Big Time because they were one of his best and biggest customers. He did not want to alienate them in any way that could lead to his losing their account. He committed to pay Mach 1 Funding the whole amount due.

Over the next few months, he started making some payments from the reserves of his funded invoices towards the Big Time account debt. Two to three months after that incident, David submitted a $30,000 invoice to another customer, Cross Town Contractors. However, after a few months of persistent follow-up, he admitted the work for which the Cross Town invoice was billed had not been completed, and would not be completed until few months later.

I contacted Cross Town's owner, Willie Payup, who confirmed the incomplete work. I reminded Willie that this violated his acknowledgment of the invoice which stated explicitly that the work had been fully and satisfactorily performed, and that our funding had been provided based on the truthfulness of this acknowledgement. Willie agreed he would pay the balance of $6,000 once the work was completed several months from then.

 A month or so after I spoke with Willie, David came to my office and pleaded for $10,000 in order to meet payroll. He unequivocally promised to pay it back within 14 days at which time he would have an invoice ready to fund to replace the $10,000. We provided him with the money after signing the proper paperwork. David never paid it back.

 At that point, I started a rigorous follow-up with David by phone, certified mail, and faxes. David stopped responding. After a series of escalating follow-up messages, David called at a time when he knew that my office was closed, and left a message on my voice mail saying, in effect, he could not pay any debt. Furthermore, if I sued him, he would declare bankruptcy. I sued him and he declared bankruptcy. At that time he owed me more than $115,000.

Thus after almost three years of factoring a total amount close to $1.5 million, a client that started in an exemplary fashion ended up in a bankruptcy and with a lawsuit filed against him for fraud. Obviously, that was a culmination of several big mistakes made by the client as well as by me, the factor.

To summarize, David's three major administrative mistakes were:

 1. Accepting larger jobs with smaller margins, and paying too much for marketing.

 2. Accepting jobs which paid slower and thereby increased his factoring charges, lowering his profit margin even more.

 3. Accepting fewer smaller jobs with good margins over the larger, less profitable jobs.

Other mistakes David made included untruthful actions, such as:

 1. Submitting invoices with offsets, yet not telling Mach 1 these offsets existed.

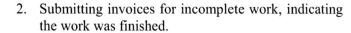

2. Submitting invoices for incomplete work, indicating the work was finished.

3. Pleading for $10,000 for payroll, promising to pay it back in short order, which never happened.

As far as my mistakes as a factor in this case, they are reflected in the following lessons that I have learned from this episode:

1. Keep up your contacts at all times with account debtors – decision makers and A/P officers.

2. Do not let your guard down.

3. Pick up on "red flags" or symptoms that something is wrong: delayed payments, continuous cash shortages, false statements, etc.

4. Do not depart from common sense. Whatever the client promises, even with the best of intentions, make sure it makes sense.

5. Monitor your client's account and look for changes in volume, payment patterns, customer concentration, etc.

6. Do not count on the legal system to protect you.

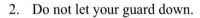

+   +   +

Analysis

This is a great example of what an otherwise good client will do when his back is against the wall.

David started his factoring relationship with problems: a large debt to his former partner plus a monthly cash drain to an IRS lien. Mach 1 Funding rode in on a white horse with shining armor, providing funds to overcome these difficult obligations. But the impression was no doubt made on David (as is often the case with factoring clients) that Mach 1 had ample funds while David didn't, and Mach 1 would have funds in the future, even when David didn't. You can probably see the seeds being sown in David's mind, "I need this money more than that rich factor."

When the going got tough (due to his own unwise management decisions), David "ran scared" and defrauded Mach 1. How? He twice withheld information about factored invoices. First he factored invoices with offsets, then he factored invoices in which the work was incomplete, indicating all services were finished. Both times he presented the invoices as valid, due, and payable in full, which was untrue. That's fraud.

Unfortunately, a client's dishonesty has a way of sooner or later catching up with both the deceitful business owner, and the unsuspecting factor trying to help.

Risks exemplified in this case study include the following

1. Poor management by the client including:
    - Growing too fast to manage properly.
    - Paying too much for marketing staff.
    - Taking larger jobs with less profit margin and slower payment.
    - Refusing smaller jobs with larger profit margin and faster payment.
    - Requesting funds to meet payroll from advances for work not yet complete. I wonder: did he *really* expect to be able to pay this loan back? I have my doubts.

2. Fraud committed by this client:
    - Submitting invoices with offsets, but not disclosing the offsets to Mach 1.
    - Submitting invoices with incomplete work, saying all work was done.
    Nonpayment from the customer resulted from the client's fraud.

3. Mistakes by the factor included:
    - Funding invoices without verifying all work was complete. More careful due diligence probably would have deterred the problems that followed.
    - Loaning money to a client in financial trouble, who already owes substantial funds due to unpaid or fraudulent invoices. This is one of the

most costly mistakes a small factor can make. Despite their desperation and pleading in such difficult situations, small factors are wise to remember the immortal words of Nancy Reagan: "Just say, 'No.'"

4

Slippery Cliff
International Press

Slippery Cliff International Press (SCIP) was a commercial printer that specialized in custom coloring books distributed as giveaways by their customers during certain seasons or events such as Christmas, Easter, Poison Prevention month, etc. Customers included shopping malls, government agencies such as forestry and fire departments, sheriff's departments, airports, supermarkets, museums, farms, and so on.

SCIP was the customer of one of my existing clients, which is a printing press. SCIP was outsourcing its printing to my client and when the owner, Cliff Trickey, saw the benefits my client was getting from factoring, he approached me to factor his own invoices and purchase orders. We signed him up in April.

Within three to four months signs of trouble started:

- There was a problem with SCIP in paying invoices as an account debtor to my client. Eventually they paid in installments over several months.
- It turned out that, contrary to what they led me to believe, all they wanted funded were purchase orders rather than invoices.
- I started having difficulty reaching Cliff. He always had excuses not to see me because of extensive travel, non-stop meetings, sickness, working very hard etc.

To remedy the problem of purchase orders, I instituted the procedure that purchase orders with more than 30 day deliveries would not be factored and that SCIP must buy back any purchase order/invoice which had been outstanding for more than 60 days.

Because of the nature of the commercial printing industry, particularly the customer proofreading and job approval procedures, purchase orders usually take a long time to deliver. Therefore our 60 day buyback period did not work. We had to extend it to 90 days and consequently raise the funding limit which I imposed on SCIP.

 By the fourth month of dealing with SCIP, it was abundantly clear that Cliff was not reliable and was not capable of keeping his promises.

 My first major mistake was not being strict in enforcing our agreements. Many purchase orders/invoices started to remain outstanding for more than 90 days and some extended several months. I kept following up with Cliff verbally and in writing to diligently pursue collections from his customers[1]. I reminded him that such delays in payments were substantially increasing his cost and reducing his profits, defeating the purpose of factoring. His response was always that his customers were great, but slow paying, as is mostly the case in this industry. He also insisted that he did not mind paying high discounts in order to expand his business because his profit margin of about 80% could accommodate such costs.

 I went along with his arguments; that was my second major mistake. My justification was that, although the purchase orders/invoices were outstanding for long periods of time, they were eventually being paid, and yes, SCIP was growing and acquiring new customers. By the end of that year, we had already funded about 50 purchase orders/invoices averaging about $7,000 per invoice. We received a testimonial from Cliff stating his excitement about our funding program which helped him "offer terms our customers need at a rate we can afford" and enabled him to "increase production while lowering the delivery time to our customers."

---

[1] At this point the factor should be making the collection calls, not relying on the client (who has proven to be unreliable) to do so.

As time went on, payments were getting slower and slower to the point that some purchase orders/invoices were outstanding for more than one year. I started giving Cliff incentives to close such invoices by reducing the earned discounts by 50% and by reducing the discount once he brought and maintained all of his outstanding invoices to less than 90 days. He was never able to take advantage of such offers. That should have been a red flag. I offered to have Mach 1 pursue collections with his customers to save him time and money. He adamantly opposed this on the grounds that it would alienate his customers and that he would pay me to the last penny. Accepting this situation was my third and possibly the single biggest mistake.

By August the state of the account was getting worse. My regular monthly meetings with Cliff were dwindling because of his avoidance. It was getting more and more difficult to obtain from Cliff a response on the weekly delivery schedule that we regularly sent him.

His response to my continuous stream of letters, reporting to him in detail the status of his account and prompting him to perform, was very difficult to come by. I tried several ways, using the stick and carrot approach: threatening with cutting funds, reporting to credit agencies, taking legal action, etc. On the other hand, I tried giving him sizable discounts, offering him more incentives, responding favorably to his requests of increased funding levels, paying advances to him rather than his vendors, accepting his wishes not to contact his customers, etc.

By the end of the next year we had already funded another 106 purchase orders/invoices averaging about $4,000 per invoice. All this time, for almost two years, I maintained that Cliff was an honest, hardworking man. His major problem was mismanagement and lack of organization and discipline.

It was not until the middle of the next year that I started noticing some suspicious transactions and behavior:

- Submission of duplicate invoices to be funded.
- Receiving from Cliff checks that bounced.

- Accepting from Cliff postdated checks (to assure me of future payments and put my mind at ease) that we were never able to deposit.
- Not receiving checks from his account debtors in our mail box for more than 3 months.

I still did not want to believe (or was afraid to admit to myself) that there was foul play. I tried to believe Cliff's explanations and promises.

On August 23 of the third year we received a phone call from a fire department complaining that SCIP had delivered only 20,000 books eight months ago and never delivered the remaining balance of 50,000 books although they were paid in full more than six months earlier. They threatened legal action against SCIP. I immediately contacted Cliff who firmly and unequivocally assured me that he did not receive a single penny from the customer and that he would take care of the problem.

At that time, we asked the fire department for a copy of the cashed check and, to our shock and dismay, we received it, showing that SCIP had deposited the check more than six months earlier.

I started taking immediate action:

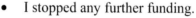

- I stopped any further funding.
- I confronted Cliff with his fraudulent action, and sent him a copy of the signed agreement stipulating the consequences of such actions.
- We started, for the first time, contacting all the customers of SCIP. We found out that some of them already paid SCIP a long time ago; others had recently sent checks, and others had not yet paid.

For those who paid a long time ago, we asked for a copy of the cashed check. Then we requested they pay us in accordance with their signed acknowledgements which stated that any payment not made to us, at our address, was not considered payment. Two of those customers recognized their mistake, and promptly paid us. We pursued the others until we eventually reached a settlement with SCIP that covered those payments.

For those who had sent their checks recently, we asked them to stop payment on those checks and redirect their payments to us. We were able to successfully interrupt several such payments. For those who had not yet paid, we requested that payments be directed to us as per their acknowledgement. Thus, we were able to collect several payments.

All in all, our immediate action resulted in collections of over $50,000; we were not able to collect the remaining $150,000 because the majority of orders were not delivered by SCIP.

A new agreement was signed by Cliff committing to a plan of repayment to Mach 1. Furthermore, Cliff submitted a $50,000 purchase order from a very well known big pharmacy chain, for which Mach 1 would keep all the proceeds. We took full control of the order and were able to realize an additional $15,000 that was applied to Cliff's debt.

Cliff again was not able to fulfill his payment commitments to us, which led us to send his account to a collection agency. We were lucky. The collection agency was able to collect $150,000 from Cliff, which was directed to us after we gladly paid the agency its well-deserved fee. Thus after factoring about 200 invoices totaling about $1 million over a period of about three years, we were able, by luck more than anything else, to come out of a very bad deal, with a good financial result.[2]

As is clearly obvious from the above, we made numerous major mistakes on this account. I believe we made more mistakes on this account than any other. We were lucky to collect much more than we expected, and we learned very valuable lessons:

1. Keep your contacts at all times with account debtors.
2. Enforce your own terms and rules.

---

[2] Most factors are not nearly as fortunate in such situations.

3. Limit period of outstanding invoices (maybe 30 to 120 days maximum).

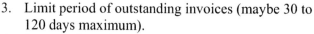

4. In case of purchase orders, make sure that advances are directly paid to the vendors, not to the client.

5. Limit your overall exposure.
6. Look out for trouble signs and take immediate action. Such signs include:

   - complete opposition by client to contact his customers
   - slow or delayed payments
   - duplicate invoicing
   - delayed shipments

7. Do not depart from common sense. Whatever the client promises, even with the best of intentions, make sure it makes sense.

8. Monitor, monitor, monitor…and verify, verify, verify.

+ + +

Analysis

As Mike acknowledges, he made some serious mistakes and was very lucky to come out as well as he did here.

First, he factored a business that was a customer for an existing client. In *Factoring Small Receivables* this is called "chaining clients" and is a two-edged sword. As long as both clients' accounts perform smoothly, things are fine. But if one account falters, the domino effect can ruin both accounts and cost you dearly as a factor.

Any time a client becomes difficult to reach and payments are slow coming in, beware. Even more, take firm control of the account, especially collection calls. When you leave collections solely in the hands of a client who has become a distressed account, you are inviting problems.

This case argues against factoring very slow paying customers. Thirty to forty-five, even sixty day payers, are one thing. But when payments go over ninety days – in this case a *year* – there is little benefit to either the factor or the client to buy such customers' invoices.

Likewise, when a client isn't concerned about his factoring discount getting high from very slow payments, something is wrong. No good business owner will brush off ever-increasing costs which result in ever-decreasing profits. They will accept expected discounts for normal waits, but will start to agonize over high discounts from exceedingly slow payments. If they don't, something's askew.

Another telling aspect of this case is Mike's reluctance to "smell a rat." Such denial is common among factors who have integrity. They tend to assume their clients are also people with integrity. Yet just one experience with a "Slippery Cliff" will make you much more cautious – even suspicious – thereafter. When Mike finally realized Cliff's "M.O." and took immediate action, he did all the right things. Unfortunately he didn't do them sooner.

One final issue in this case is over-concentration. When Mike finally pulled the plug on Cliff he was owed around $200,000. This suggests Mike was over-concentrated in this client. It's a good idea to invest no more than 10% of your funds in any client. Following that formula, Mike would need $2 million in factoring funds to avoid being over-concentrated with SCIP.

The fastest way to go out of business as a factor is to have too many eggs in one basket (clients, customers, and invoices included). If Mike's collection agency had collected zero or even as much as $25,000 or $50,000 instead of $150,000, the future of Mach 1 Funding may have turned out quite differently…and not as happily.

5

MagicAl Garments International

MagicAl Garments International (MAGI) is a small company that designs and supplies specialty garments to retail stores and military cooperatives.

MAGI was referred to me by one of my brokers. After some due diligence, we found this to be a one-man company owned by Al Gonn – who was almost penniless. However, Al had a $50,000 valid purchase order from the Air Force Cooperative (AAFES).

I did not have any experience in factoring invoices of the garment industry, let alone funding the trickier and riskier purchase order. But I really felt I should help Al, because I saw in him a person struggling to make a living and he was desperate not to lose this opportunity. He had connections at the purchasing department of AAFES, which availed him of this opportunity. If he failed, chances were next to nil he would get another such opportunity. If he provided the product on time there would be many more orders on the way.

I realized the extreme importance of this opportunity to Al, who desperately pleaded for help, and I was intent to oblige. After all, there was enough profit margin in this transaction to allow for purchase order funding and factoring discounts and still leave a healthy profit for Al.

I did some research that led me to Phil Hazpull, a "consultant" who specialized in fulfilling purchase orders for the garment industry. Phil related to me horror stories of deceit and fraud in this industry. His basic strategy in dealing with such transactions is to take full control of the transaction and not to allow the client to even touch the product. That is, the product is completely out of the control of the client from manufacturing to warehousing to sale.

Phil asked for 5% of the value of the purchase order to handle the transaction. Although this represented more than 50% of my discount, I accepted in order to get the job done properly. So I signed MAGI in late December.

Phil took control of the transaction indeed. He contacted my client as well as all his vendors. He coordinated the shipments from all five vendors to a central warehouse. I issued checks to the different vendors only upon instructions from Phil. Once all the merchandise was delivered to the warehouse from all the vendors, the warehouse (which specializes in such operations) completed the job of labeling, packing, boxing, and shipping to AAFES in accordance with their precise instructions.

Upon verification of delivery to AAFES, I issued checks to the warehouse and to Phil. At this time, the purchase order transaction was complete and a factoring transaction was created.

Since the factoring advance is higher than the purchase order funding advance plus the corresponding charge, Al received his first cash installment. Noting that he received cash for a zero investment (i.e., infinite Return on Investment), Al enjoyed his new designation as a "MagicAl."

When AAFES paid the invoice in full within 30 days, Al received another cash installment (his reserve), which completed the factoring transaction. Thus Al made a total of about $15,000 in less than two months with a zero investment.

Needless to say, Al was simply elated, I got an extremely high sense of satisfaction and everybody was happy – Phil, the vendors, AAFES, Al, and me. It was truly a win-win situation for everybody concerned.

Three to four months later, Al factored another $25,000 invoice to the same customer. This time, however, he did not need purchase order funding, which definitely gave him an even higher profit margin. It seems with some cash at hand

and newly acquired credibility with his vendors, he managed to put the order together and pay his vendors from the proceeds of factoring.

Although the hardest and costliest lessons are learned from bad experiences, I am a firm believer that one could learn from all experiences, including the good ones. Some of what we have learned from this account:

1. Caring for people pays off.
2. Do not discard opportunities without thoroughly examining the situation. I am willing to bet, with anyone who cares to lose, that such a transaction would have been turned down by the great majority of funding sources.

3. Do your homework. Research and get help when you need it; it is better to do things right and accept less profit than take the risk of doing things wrong for a higher expected profit.

+ + +

Analysis

Mike was fortunate he could rely on Phil's expertise to guide him through every step of this potentially mine-infested transaction. If Mike had factored this deal without Phil's guidance and instructions, this story may well have ended less happily.

After all, when Mike came to the table Al was "almost penniless" and certainly could never have paid Mike back if the deal had soured. If you get cleaned out and are looking for your money back, personal guarantees and other legal documents mean very little with clients in such a condition.

Fortunately this story has a happy ending and everyone smiled all the way to the bank. Al was able to factor future invoices without future purchase order funding, which is always the goal.

Notice Mike's three closing pieces of advice. "Caring for people pays off" as this story so aptly illustrates. This is another example of Mike's excellent customer service reaping rewards for everyone. What's more, pay careful attention when a deal crosses your desk that is "undesirable" to most people. Others would have turned this down with good reason: without a Phil in their camp they could have taken a bath.

Finally, Mike found Phil after doing some research. This deal required homework and Mike did it, which landed Phil on his team. Especially important, Mike was willing to pay Phil what he was worth – which was more than half of Mike's income on this deal. If Mike had been greedy and wanted the entire income for himself, he could have lost a bundle. Instead, Mike's common sense prevailed and everybody won.

Condor International Financial Services

Contact Information
Condor International Financial Services
Richard Shapiro, President
4725 E. Sunrise Dr. Suite. 148
Tucson, AZ 85718
Phone: (520) 529-4960
Fax: (520) 299-3450
Email: condor@condorfunding.com
Web Site: www.condorfunding.com

Richard Shapiro

Richard Shapiro is the owner of Condor International Financial Services and entered the cash flow industry in October of 1994 after completing the International Factoring Institute training. He later became a Diversified Cash Flow Specialist after completing the DCFS Program given by the American Cash Flow Association (ACFA).

He has been a Master Broker in factoring for the ACFA since 1998, and was an instructor for the Pino Training Organization. Richard is a regular contributor to the *American Cash Flow Journal*® and other national and local publications. He is a regular presenter along with his wife, Kendall SummerHawk, at the annual Cash Flow conventions. He is also Chairman of the Tucson Chapter of the ACFA.

Born and raised in New York City, Richard graduated from the State University of New York at Albany. He has led a varied and, he says, not too interesting career path. He did a short stint (15 years) as a handyman. His motto was and is, "If it ain't broke, I'll fix it. If it is broke, that costs extra."

He has owned and operated a number of businesses in Tucson. He has been an investor in start up companies as well as buying and selling real estate notes. Other activities include membership in and President of Inventors Association of Arizona, Inc.; former member Arizona Small Business Association; participant in the Tucson Chapter of "Brain Trust" Development; member of the Tucson Sailing Club[1]; and member of Pima Trails Association.

Richard specializes in brokering transactions and assisting other brokers in factoring and purchase order financing, as well as funding for future contracts. He also brokers business notes, real estate notes, structured settlements, lottery winnings, and asset based lending. As you can see he also occasionally purchases small receivables. Richard has branched out to mentoring others in another specialty, pre-settlement lawsuit funding. He teaches TeleClasses and is a frequent speaker at local and not-so-local events.

Richard and Kendall live on the outskirts of Tucson in their adobe abode on two acres of dust and cactus with their three cats, two horses, Gila monster and other critters of the desert too numerous to mention. When not helping others achieve success you can find this happy couple riding the trails and washes of their desert home. In the evening when they are not sitting around the fire ring by the chuck wagon strumming their guitars and serenading each other and the harvest moon, they will be found burning up the hardwood floors of the local saloons and dance halls with their fancy footwork.

---

[1] Yes, there really is a sailing club in Tucson.

6

Lack of Moolah
Construction Suppliers

This is a factoring transaction that had a bit of a rocky start, but turned out working for everybody. It was a "spot factoring" deal – a one-time transaction.

A business associate of mine, who is Lack of Moolah's attorney, introduced me to the client, Lack of Moolah Construction Suppliers. Lack of Moolah had a patented insulated building panel that they were marketing locally, with plans to develop a number of manufacturing sites around the country. Part of their patents included the machinery to build the panels.

The 8 foot wide and up to 16 foot long panels were built in the factory to specifications of the architect for the roof and the exterior walls. The thickness could be made anywhere from 3.5 inches to 11.25 inches to create walls that were similar to dimensional framing. They were then delivered to the prepared slab, and a crew could have the entire shell of the house up in a day or two. The savings in labor more than made up for the added expense of the panels. Because they were super-insulated the savings in energy costs gave these panels a competitive edge.

Through the attorney they were trying to raise expansion capital in the venture market place. They had a letter of commitment from a venture group that was going to fund in about 60 days. They needed working capital to get them through to the funding. They had a receivable they wanted to use as collateral. They had tried their bank, but had been turned down. The bank had previously loaned them money against their home to start the business, but did not want to commit any more money into this two-year old company. This is where I came in.

Lack of Moolah's invoice was about $60,000. However, the customer, Fly By Night Builders, was in trouble and was going to file for bankruptcy. Fly By Night had bought six lots in a new upscale development. They had completed one house and had the slab poured for this second one when the trouble surfaced from a previous project. Half of the panels for this house were already delivered to the site, but were not set up. The other half of the panels were sitting in Lack of Moolah's yard.

The homeowner was understandably distraught, because their dream house looked like it was never going to get built. Lack of Moolah was hurting for working capital and was facing the possibility of closing down their operation temporarily, which probably would have killed their venture deal as well.

Happy Face Developers was faced with the possibility of a chain link fence going up around five of their lots in the middle of their upscale planned community. Not only would this have been an eyesore, but also it might have created a bad image for the whole project.

Happy Face Developers, Fly By Night, and Good Hammer Enterprises (another builder who had bought lots in the same development) went through around-the-clock negotiations to work out something that would not tie up these lots in the courts for months if not years. Finally, Fly By Night was out and Good Hammer was in, which gave everybody a chance to move forward.

Good Hammer was willing to sign for the entire set of panels once the second half were delivered. Lack of Moolah delivered the panels later that week. We were able to get a sign off[2] from Good Hammer, and I funded Lack of Moolah the next day. The homeowners were happy to see their home underway again. Good Hammer was able to take over

---

[2] That is, Good Hammer became the customer for the panels invoice and Condor verified Good Hammer would pay the full amount of the invoice to Condor.

another 5 lots with virtually nothing out of their pocket. Happy Face Developers was happy because his project was moving along again towards completion, and Lack of Moolah was happy because they had the money they needed to get them through to the permanent funding.

Oh yeah, I was happy too about 53 days later when the invoice was paid in full and I gave Lack of Moolah their rebate.

+   +   +

Analysis

This case study shows how factors can help make transactions happen which, as Richard pointed out, otherwise would likely have ended tied up in court and been a neighborhood eyesore for years. Instead, everyone involved came out winners including Richard. In this case, Condor lived up to the meaning of the word "factor": "one who makes it happen."

7

Outtasight Imports, Unlimited

This is a factoring transaction that started out as a good relationship for both the client and me. Events changed all that.

Outtasight Imports, Unlimited was a business that resulted from the efforts of the young entrepreneur, Irving Mordachai (I. M.) Hy, to change his enterprise from a dealer of undeclared goods into a legitimate importer.

As a youth of the 1960's I.M. had spent a great deal of time on the Indian Subcontinent, in pursuit of spiritual enlightenment or whatever, mostly whatever. To carry his undeclared goods into this country, he had to secret them into goods he could declare. Once in the USA, he would dispose of both the declared and undeclared at a handsome profit. Our carefree youth went on like this for years. Eventually things changed. He got married, and soon thereafter twins blessed the Hy household. (You do not have to do the math; she was!)

I.M. decided it was time to go straight. Since he was already bringing in goods, mostly wooden carvings and furniture from India that sold quickly, he decided to build on this. At first he was selling out of his garage. The business grew to the point where he rented a mini storage. Eventually he rented a storefront in an old warehouse. He started getting requests from other retailers which led him to begin selling wholesale.

As a retailer, he knew he would get paid the same day either in cash or through credit cards (Sorry No Checks Accepted). As a wholesaler, he had to extend terms. Since most of his earlier profits had "gone up in smoke," and because his business as well as his family and his waistline were growing rapidly, he had a perpetual major cash flow "situation." A mutual friend introduced us. After explaining slowly four or five times how factoring worked, I.M. agreed to go forward. We contracted with him and started buying invoices.

Things went along well. Occasionally we would have a "challenge" with one of his customers, but for the most part we were all happy.

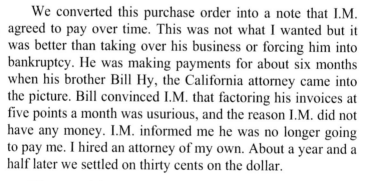

One day, I.M. came to me with a substantial purchase order from "Cute, Useless and Cheap" a well-known retail chain. I was new to the purchase order funding world ("We don't need no stinkin' insurance! Letter of Credit? What's that, man?") but decided to go ahead with it. He wired the order to his suppliers in India along with my money. Did I mention my money? Oh yeah, and OH YEAH!!!

The monsoon season came on with a vengeance that year. Not only was it raining cats and dogs; it came down in buckets of holy cows. The wood would not dry. Very few woodchucks were chucking wood. Any product that was made could not be shipped because the roads were washed out. Water leaking through the roof, windows and doors was damaging the finished goods that were piling up at the factory. The long and the short of it: he could not fill the purchase order on time and it was cancelled.

We converted this purchase order into a note that I.M. agreed to pay over time. This was not what I wanted but it was better than taking over his business or forcing him into bankruptcy. He was making payments for about six months when his brother Bill Hy, the California attorney came into the picture. Bill convinced I.M. that factoring his invoices at five points a month was usurious, and the reason I.M. did not have any money. I.M. informed me he was no longer going to pay me. I hired an attorney of my own. About a year and a half later we settled on thirty cents on the dollar.

The moral here is to work with honest people doing things you understand, and in a dollar amount you can afford (to lose!)

+   +   +

Analysis

This case study shows the hazards into which inexperienced factors can unknowingly wander, where seasoned veterans would wisely not tread.

The first risk: I.M. Hy's lifestyle was not exactly conducive to long-term profitability and sound business decisions. Much of his profits went "up in smoke" and his business acumen (if he had much to start with) was further clouded.

Next, Richard found himself financing a transaction in which he had no experience (risk two), which was a non-government purchase order (risk three) involving a foreign (risk four) supplier. Such a risk-laced transaction had a greater chance of failing than succeeding, but due to Richard's inexperience at this point in his career, he did not recognize this.

Such naiveté illustrates three truths new factors must remember.

1) Factors make mistakes (just like this) in their early transactions, and these mistakes end up costing money. Therefore, keep those first transactions very small so the potential loss is minimized. As Richard put it, work with dollar amounts "you can afford (to lose)."

2) If you have no clue what you are doing with "exotic" transactions like these, don't go near them. Stick with the more familiar and ordinary. They may seem mundane, but your chances of getting burned are considerably less.

3) New factors need to get into the habit of asking of every new client: "What can go wrong here that can result in the loss of my money?" With Outtasight Imports there were numerous risks:

a) Foreign suppliers who were subject to innumerable distant and climatic conditions.

b) A dishonest business owner who started his company illegally smuggling products into the U.S.

c) A business owner with little or no integrity as to making good on a legitimate debt to the person who helped him.

d) A business owner who acted reactively rather than proactively…and often "under the influence," at that.

e) A purchase order transaction which Richard acknowledges he "did not understand."

Be sure you are clear as to what is happening with your money and that it will be used as you intend. Once Richard wired his funds to India, he had zero control over it. If you feel like you're putting your money in a black hole, there's a high probability that's exactly where it will go…and stay.

8

NoGoodnicks.com

This is a factoring transaction that is the epitome of dishonesty. I was set up.

NoGoodnicks.com was a company that did web hosting, marketing and other Internet related business. I met Izzy Real the president of NG.com at a networking event. He said his company was growing quickly and he needed funding. His business was new so the banks were not interested in talking to him. We made plans to meet at his office to discuss the possibilities of buying his invoices.

Before the meeting he showed me around his place. There were servers and computers and wires all over the place. The phones were ringing and people were going back and forth at the speed of the Internet. I must admit, I was impressed.

We finally sat down in his office, and he showed me his receivables. There were three invoices of about $5,000 each from companies whose names I recognized as being long time local businesses. There was one for about $3,000 to a company Here-Today-Gone-Tomorrow.net (HTGT.net, or "HitGut.net") that I did not recognize. When I did a little checking into it, Here-Today-Gone-Tomorrow.net was a brand new company.

A few days later after we had completed all our paperwork and filings, I decided to risk it and bought all the invoices. I sent out Notices of Assignment to all the customers. They all came back to me signed. To my surprise the invoice to Here-Today-Gone-Tomorrow.net was paid in a matter of days. A day or two later, another invoice to Here-Today-Gone-Tomorrow.net was submitted, this time for about $5,000. Again the Notice of Assignment was sent and Here-Today-Gone-Tomorrow.net signed it and sent it back to me. Amazingly enough, the invoice paid again in a matter of just a few days.

About a month later the other three invoices paid. Things were going great. Not only was this turning into a really easy account, Izzy was a great golfer. He took me out for a round of golf and gave me some "free" lessons.

About a month later Izzy submitted some more invoices that averaged about $2-3,000 each and one to HTGT.net for $15,000. Again all the Notices of Assignment were sent out, signed off and sent back to me. Again the invoice to Here-Today-Gone-Tomorrow.net was paid in less then a week. Izzy had taken me out to lunch. I had invited him over for a dinner party. We were getting to be buddies. The rest of the invoices paid off in about five weeks.

Shortly after that Izzy called me to tell me he had a chance to buy some equipment real cheap from a company that was going out of business. It had to be with cash and it had to be in a day or two or he would lose the deal. If he could get this equipment he could improve his business ten fold and make a ton of money. I told him that is not what I do. He said he had made a big sale to Here-Today-Gone-Tomorrow.net. It was for $25,000. I told him I would be happy to buy that from him since all my other transactions with them had gone smoothly.

DD I sent out the Notice of Assignment to Here-Today-Gone-Tomorrow.net. I got a voice message back that Howie Cheatum, the owner of Here-Today-Gone-Tomorrow.net was out of the country and would not return until next week. I called Izzy and told him what was going on. He pleaded with me to advance the money so he could buy the equipment. He made a good argument that since all the deals with Here-Today-Gone-Tomorrow.net worked out well, why shouldn't this one? I advanced the money without getting a sign off.

A week went by and I tried to contact Howie. He did not return my calls. I mailed out a copy of the Notice of Assignment to him. It was returned unopened. I called Izzy to tell him the problems I was having with this deal. Instead of getting the receptionist, the phone was answered by

NoGoodnicks.com's messaging system. Izzy never returned any of my calls.

About a week later, I drove over to NoGoodnicks.com's office. There was a "For Rent" sign in the window. I drove out to Izzy's apartment. He had moved. When I called his cell phone, I was put into voice messaging. I never heard from Izzy again.

Since I never got a sign off from Here-Today-Gone-Tomorrow.net, they are not responsible for paying me. I am now in the process of trying to enforce the personal guarantee by filing a suit against Izzy in Superior Court. I may get a judgment that is uncollectable. This may force him into bankruptcy some day. Or he may see the error of his ways and send me a certified check and a pass for 18 holes of golf at his favorite course.

I am not holding my breath.

+   +   +

Analysis

Wow. This is the client of your nightmares: the professional crook who intentionally sets you up by gaining your confidence (with a few quick-paying invoices to start), and even earns your friendship (golf lessons and a dinner party). He plays the game just long enough to set the table, invite you to sit down…and then yanks the chair out from under you.

One of the most dangerous red flags here is Izzy's pressuring Richard:

1) to provide a larger amount of cash than he ever had earlier,
2) to provide it immediately, and
3) the threat that if he didn't provide it, a brief and rare window of opportunity to make a windfall profit would close.

Izzy is not only appealing to Richard's friendship and trust, he is also appealing to a part of human nature against which every factor must be forever vigilant: his sense of greed. Richard will make a tidy sum if he just bends his rules a little and helps out his golfing buddy, Izzy. Aw, c'mon Richard, old pal....

Never allow yourself to be pressured!! If you are pressured and you feel uncomfortable, *follow your instincts.* Remember again Nancy Reagan: "Just say, 'No.'" Firmly. If your newfound "buddy" turns on you for refusing his request, he is nothing more than a wolf in sheep's clothing. Be glad you've discovered the truth about his "friendship," and that you haven't lost any money in the process.

This case study also argues for keeping your transactions small and credit limits modest for yet another reason. Sophisticated crooks are more likely to try larger scams than smaller ones. If you are suckered into a small one (which you probably will be sooner or later), you lose less. If you fall for a big one – which can happen very easily – your loss can be catastrophic.

9

Happy Helping Hands Temporary Agency

This is a factoring transaction that is the epitome of what factoring can do for a company. This was a long-term relationship (five years) that grew stronger with time as the client grew stronger.

Happy Helping Hands (HHH) was a temporary agency that was brought to me by a broker named Georgio Gobetweeno (GG). HHH was a husband and wife owned business. The wife took care of most of the upfront office chores, and the husband did all the back room duties. Before I became involved with them, they were using No Problems Please Funding, (NPPF, another factor) for their sole form of financing. Everybody was happy with this situation.

Without warning, dark clouds formed quickly. A storm broke in the form of a computer glitch. HHH had not been withholding enough for payroll taxes. When they got the notice they realized there was no way to make up the deficit in a timely fashion. At the same time when NPPF heard about HHH's problem the NPPF pulled out giving HHH no time to finance that week's receivables. HHH had only one choice. They filed for bankruptcy protection so they could work out a reorganization plan. Their doors were closed for almost a week while they scrambled to save their company.

Georgio brought in another factoring company, Big Invoices Only, LLC (BIO). HHH opened their doors again, but business was slow. It was almost like starting from scratch. It may have been even worse because the word was out that HHH was in financial trouble. It was almost as hard to get temps to sign up with them, as it was to get their customers back. BIO was not happy with $500 to $1,000 a week in total invoicing, with individual invoices being as low as $50. BIO informed HHH that they were pulling out. Georgio had heard of me through my networking efforts. Since I was a small factor and was located locally he gave me a call. This was towards the end of the year.

HHH, Georgio and I sat down and worked out an arrangement that would make me the accounts receivable department for HHH. I was going to finance every one of their invoices at a 70% advance and a discount of 2.5 points for each 15 days. We took the plan to the Trustee and it was approved.

At first the invoicing was less than $1,000 a week. As time wore on, they slowly built their business back. By spring, they were doing about $5,000 per week. By the end of the summer, it was closer to $7,500. By the end of the following year they were doing up to $10,000 per week. They asked for an increase in the advance and I gave it to them. I increased the advance to 75%. By summer of the next year they were doing $15,000 per week. At their request I gave them another increase of the advance to 80%. My final move two years later was an increase to 85% when their invoicing hit $22,000 per week.

At this time they had just about worked themselves out of the bankruptcy. They had been looking around and found New York City Boos (NYCB), another factor that offered them 85% and a 3 point discount for 30 days. They asked me if I wanted to match it. I did not want to so they switched over. HHH had been my "bread and butter" account for 3 years. Now they were gone.

But wait! This is not the end of the story.

The honeymoon ended quickly. HHH became unhappy with NYCB in part because I had been easy to work with and partially because of the difference in time zones. HHH called me up to see if I wanted to take them on again. I told them I could not match the rates and terms they currently had. They asked me if I could find somebody locally who would be willing to match the rates and terms. I ended up brokering HHH to Diversified Dried Desert Discounters (DDDD). I receive a brokerage commission every month, which I split with the original broker. It is not the same as when I funded HHH but it still spends the same.

+ + +

Analysis

Here we see the value of the excellent service a small factor can provide, compared to the less personalized service of larger factoring companies. The big companies' names here fit too many larger factors to a "T": No Problems Please and Big Invoices Only. Small, local factors are usually the best match for small businesses as this case study shows. In time HHH simply outgrew Condor, but that is a mark of success for both of them.

Notice the biggest problem arose from an administrative error HHH made in reporting payroll taxes. A prudent move when factoring temp agencies is to require them to use a payroll service. If HHH had, this error would not have happened. When a payroll service is used and you receive proof on a regular basis that payroll taxes are being paid properly, and employees are receiving paychecks properly, your risk with temp agencies is drastically reduced. When that's the case, and a temp agency grows like this one did – which is not unusual – everyone can make a very tidy profit.

Prime Time Funding, Inc.

Contact Information
Prime Time Funding, Inc.
Ron Weber, President
PO Box 70563
Reno, NV 89570-0563
Phone: 775-345-2785
Fax: 775-345-2790
Email: ptfron@yahoo.com

Ron Weber

Ron Weber earned an engineering degree from Southwest Minnesota State University and an MBA degree from Mankato State University in Minnesota. He worked for 4 years at Hormel as an Industrial Engineer. After moving to Nevada in 1978, he worked for 15 years at Specialty Brands as a plant engineer and plant manager.

Ron left corporate America in 1993 and became a Certified Factoring Specialist (CFS) in January, 1994, through the International Factoring Association (now the American Cash Flow Association). He became a member of ACFA's Million Dollar Club in 1998.

Prime Time Funding, Inc. is a small factoring company that has been financing small businesses since August, 1995. Ron and his business partner, Robert Neu, factor clients starting between $100 and $15,000 in size. Ron and Robert find that offering personalized service and developing a trust with their clients makes for a good working relationship, and in turn provides referrals for future business. They believe factoring can be intimidating for a small company, so they try to make clients comfortable with the process to enable the clients to concentrate on growing their business. Prime Time Funding factors nationally and funds every industry except medical.

For eight years Ron has been a member of a local chapter of LeTip, a national networking and leads generating group, and also attends Chamber of Commerce functions. He is active in his church and has volunteered at Reno/Sparks Gospel Mission serving meals to the homeless, as well as for the American Cancer Society, giving rides for patients to their chemotherapy or radiation treatments.

During the summer Ron and his family can be found spending time away from work boating and in the water with wakeboards, water skis, and air chairs. Ron and his wife enjoy traveling and have been to Europe, China, Egypt, and Thailand in the last few years.

10

Need It Now Manufacturing

We found our first client, Need It Now Manufacturing, through my partner who received an inquiry from them when he was working for another factor. The other factor quit factoring so we followed up on the lead.

This small company consisted of the two working partners, Les Green and Shorty Cash, plus two employees, Abel Boddie and Richie Znott, and a few outside investors. We met Les and Shorty, had a good feeling about them, and felt that they were basically honest. They were here locally, so we could visit them and in most cases took their advances and reserve refunds to their office personally. That allowed us to keep a pulse on their business. What's more, they were striving to grow their business and we could discuss shortcomings.

We like to factor small manufacturing companies but they are difficult to find. If they have stellar credit and are outstanding business people, they don't need our services because they will manage their finances to get money at banks using their good personal credit. If they do not have good credit or do not have good business practices, there is a risk they may not stay in business.

Need It Now manufactured a product that could be used for industrial customers or sold to hardware and paint stores. The company's partners, Les Green and Shorty Cash, wanted to factor because they could not wait to get paid. They also wanted to sell to more customers but did not have the capital to purchase the materials to produce the goods. They wanted to factor with us because we were local and they could meet with us face to face.

Les and Shorty factored slowly at first; their first schedule was $2,800. Over time they grew to a volume of $10,000 to $15,000 per month and were our client for about three years.

We advanced 75% and charged a factoring discount of 6% for 30 days, plus 3% for the next 15 days plus 3% for the next 15 days, plus 6% for 61 to 75 days. We did not want the 6% for the 61 to 75 days, we just wanted them to help get the invoice paid by 60 days. We gave them the option to buy back their invoices at 60 days to avoid the additional discount. We gave them rebates within 10 days of a schedule closing.

We did not build up a reserve because we felt it was too restrictive for our client. We felt it was fair to give them back the reserve as a schedule was paid in full or there was enough reserve to pay off any open invoice and close the schedule. If they did have enough reserve to buy back an open invoice, we would refund that money when that payment was received from their customer.

Need It Now was valuable to us because they were small and we could learn and get our systems debugged without a huge exposure. My partner developed spreadsheets to track invoices and provide reports and close schedules.

As our relationship with Les and Shorty developed, they convinced us to lend them money to purchase a used motor home to facilitate selling at trade shows and make sales trips. The reserves from their schedules were going to be used to pay off the loan. The additional sales did not materialize so the loan was difficult for them to pay back.

Then an employee, Richie Znott, borrowed money from Les and Shorty to purchase a vehicle. Richie was unable to pay back that loan. Les gave us the title to a "collector car" to get money for personal use with the agreement to pay back our loan with reserves. Les was unable to pay back the loan and the vehicle was not really worth enough to warrant repossession and sale.

We moved to collect the outstanding debts utilizing our UCC-1 which included the equipment for the business. The investors, Manny Stocks, Lowe Dzabonds, and Fuller T. Bills, paid off the indebtedness rather than see the assets liquidated.

Les and Shorty realized the business was not generating enough cash flow to support their living expenses. Therefore, they each went on their own to obtain independent employment. They put the office manager, Abel Boddie, in charge who also had reporting duties to Manny, Lowe and Fuller. The business is back on its feet and supporting the two employees and investors.

What did we learn from Need It Now? Stick with factoring. We got into trouble when we started lending money when there were not enough invoices to satisfy their cash needs. Very often with small companies like this, the owners do not have adequate reporting to enable them to know whether they are profitable or not. With their initial systems, they were not profitable when Les and Shorty were paying their living expenses out of their business.

+   +   +

Analysis

This case study is a great example of why you should, in Ron's words, "stick with factoring" and avoid giving clients loans.

When you factor, you're relying primarily on the honesty of the client and the financial strength of the customer to pay you back. Factoring clients often have few if any financial resources, so when you rely on such people to pay you back, rather than a solid customer paying for invoices, you're taking a big chance. That's why such people can't get bank loans and need to factor: the bank has turned them down, or would if they attempted to obtain a loan. Factors accept them because of the financial strength of their customers – so why be a bank for a high-risk loan? Be a factor, and only buy their invoices.

Repaying a loan from future rebates is also high risk. Why? What happens if business slows and orders dry up? No invoices, thus no rebates, thus no loan repayment… which is exactly what happened here. Ron was fortunate that

Manny, Lowe and Fuller were there to bail out Need It Now. Otherwise, recouping the loan money would have been a long, slow process and Ron and Robert probably wouldn't have recovered all (or even any) of what they were owed.

Stick with factoring. Avoid giving loans. Minimize risk. Make more money.

Jaybec Business Funding, LLC

Contact Information
Jaybec Business Funding, LLC
Rebecca and Jay Karp
PO Box 1582
Olney, MD 20830
Tel: (301) 570-8183
Toll Free: (866) 2-JAYBEC
Fax: (301) 570-2638
E-mail: rkarp@jaybec.com
Web site: www.jaybec.com

Rebecca and Jay Karp

Rebecca and Jay Karp are Certified Mortgage Investors (CMI), Certified Factoring Specialists (CFS), and Million Dollar Club Members of the American Cash Flow Association (ACFA). They began their mortgage note business in 1994 and later decided they would rather work with business owners. Thus they started Jaybec Business Funding in 1996 after obtaining CFS status.

Rebecca joined the cash flow industry after a 25-year career in banking. Her last position was as a Senior Vice President for a New York bank, where she managed the Administrative Services departments, including Records Management, Purchasing, Systems Development and Facilities Management. Jay's experience from his parents' business as a young adult guided him through a 40-year career as an electrician. He is now retired and is in the cash flow business full time.

Intending to be factoring brokers when they started their business, Rebecca and Jay encountered several potential clients who were declined by funding sources. The reasons included size of business or other situations where the funding source did not want to participate. Since these refusals did not make much sense to Rebecca and Jay, they decided to try their hand at funding small receivables – and continue to do so today. Rebecca and Jay know they made the right decision when they receive letters and phone calls about how they have helped their clients through tight situations, and how Jaybec Business Funding has helped their clients grow their businesses and feel secure. This is a great business, they say, as long as you know your goal.

After spending all their lives in New York, the Karps now reside in Maryland. However they run their business wherever they happen to be with cell phones and a laptop. They have conducted business in California, Texas, Hawaii, and numerous other locations. While all of their clients are presently still in New York, they are concentrating their marketing efforts in Maryland.

Rebecca and Jay share four children and eight grandchildren and lots of relatives and friends throughout the U.S.

11

Hanginon Food Processing, Inc.

We met Sharon Truegrit through a previous mortgage deal in which we were involved. This story begins with Sharon as president of Hanginon Food Processing, Inc. Her company prepared unitized foods for sale to hospitals, prisons, school programs, and other such institutions. Hanginon also prepared cakes and muffins.

This was to be a new start for Sharon. She owned a successful company before from which she learned the food preparation business. Now her dream was to begin over again and not repeat earlier errors. The primary mistake she made before – only having one main customer – would not happen again. All her eggs would never again be put in one basket.

The concept was wonderful. All she needed were orders and cash to fulfill them. Then one day Sharon won a bid with the city to supply unitized dinners for hospital patients. Despite this potential boost Sharon was despondent: she had this wonderful bid but had no idea where the money would come from to fund it.

We met with her and talked about purchase order funding. Back then such transactions were a little easier than today, when purchase order funding is usually done for distributing goods that do not have to be assembled. But Sharon needed to buy the ingredients and put together the packages. There was performance here that was riskier than that of basic distribution. We set her up with Deep Pockets Capital, who was willing to provide purchase order funding, and she was off to a slow start, but a start nevertheless.

For a while, Hanginon grew slowly with Deep Pockets. As time went on, there were some problems with the relationship, and finally Sharon just stopped factoring. She didn't say why, not being one to talk badly about others, but we still stayed in touch. At one point she again talked of needing money, and we found out that she just wasn't happy with Deep Pockets.

This was the time we were beginning to look at doing our own funding, and based on her small needs, we decided that this was the way to get our feet wet. We had built a good rapport with Sharon and she was willing to go with us. We became her advisor, as well as her factor.

The food business seemed riskier because of spoilage and delivery problems. Yet in all this time, that has not been a problem. She has proven to know the food business and to be on top of all the situations that come up.

We agreed to give her a 70% advance. Our discount structure has been a 15-day charge of 3% plus an additional 2% every 15 days, averaging 4% per month after the first month.

Today, Sharon feeds day care centers, hospitals, prisons, and is starting to get requests from other states that have heard about her. She is still struggling because of an old and very large prior debt, but without factoring, she would not be in business at this point. We currently have approximately $85,000 outstanding.

There was some fraud in which Sharon was not involved that hurt us all. Individuals who were middlemen brokers for a special project required that customers pay the brokers, who were then to pay Hanginon. Against our better judgment, we funded these. These brokers sometimes took the money and ran. Our due diligence was not effective and we used emotions instead of good old-fashioned horse sense. To her credit, Sharon made good on those losses.

We funded her when she started feeding lunches to local school districts. This too proved to be a problem. The school district does not pay until it is paid by the state. The state always seems to have a reason to delay payment. These have been difficult to collect. We believe we will be paid eventually, but the slowness is hurting our cash flow.

Hanginon remains of value to us as our largest client. Sharon does a great deal of business even though she is still holding on, waiting for those one or two large contracts that will be the right ones for the business. Sharon's honesty, no matter how tough the times are for her, is a testimony to her and to our relationship. Our rapport and mutual respect is essential.

+   +   +

Analysis

This case study is a testament to Sharon's honesty and fortitude. She has been through some long and difficult financial struggles, has paid for others' dishonesty, and has stuck it out trying to make her business successful. Not all business owners would display such perseverance or integrity, as we have already seen.

Coming to know such upstanding people as Sharon, and seeing them come through such trials, is an unexpected and easily overlooked reward of factoring. The good in this human being shines through, ever so quietly.

The Karps' comment about slow payments from the school district is worth noting. While governments are the most financially stable payers out there, they can also be the slowest. What effect do such slow payments have on the small factor? In the Karps' words, "The slowness is hurting our cash flow." If your money doesn't turn consistently, dependably, and in a reasonable period of time, this is what happens:

1) You may develop a cash flow problem of your own.
2) You have less cash so you buy fewer receivables.
3) You make less in discounts.

For this reason some factors avoid government receivables – they prefer to turn their money more frequently. As you can see, government receivables that turn in 30 days are quite desirable because you have a solid payer with reasonably quick turns.

Also notice why the school districts were slow to pay: they didn't pay until they received payment from the state. When considering a new client, find out if such a waiting game (called "contingency" payments) is the case for any customer. Customers who pay contingent upon their being paid first are less desirable and sometimes higher risk than those who pay without any such "food chain" delays.

12

Lastin Line Commercial Cleaners

Moore N. Need had been in the cleaning business for some years. He was kind of a hard luck guy and things just weren't going his way. Now an opportunity came along that he couldn't resist. He bought a cleaning store in a strip mall from another fellow who had been starting to build up a trade with restoration companies. Sounded great.

Restoration companies are called in by insurance companies after fires, floods, and other disasters. They sub-contract the work that needs to be done to various companies, such as Moore's. After fires, for example, all the clothes and drapes not destroyed are cleaned to remove the odor of the fire and remove the soot.

We'd gone to a few networking group meetings where we became friendly with a bank manager, Ewell Getzip. He called one day and asked if we'd be interested in talking with Moore. Moore and Ewell were in the same strip mall and Moore went in to the bank for funding. Ewell couldn't provide a loan, but did not want to lose Moore's existing banking business.

 After meeting a few times with Moore, we decided to take a chance. Factoring his business seemed a bit riskier than we liked so we offered a 65% advance.

 Moore was delighted. He needed to fund his business and we hit it off. After a while, He learned there was more debt left behind from the seller of the business than he bargained for. The debtors were coming out of the woodwork. He worked on paying down the debt with the funding he got from me. That should have been my warning.

When a client uses factoring to pay old debts, he is not growing his business and there could be problems ahead.

For a while things went along well. Moore built up his funding to about $20,000 outstanding. His invoices were from several hundred to a few thousand dollars. The largest invoice he had was for $5,000, which was for a church,[1] mostly for draperies.

As time went on, the payments started to slow down. The restoration companies started to complain about Moore's work and started cutting down on payment. With a lot of investigation we discovered the sub-contractors doing construction work were paid first. If there was anything left, the money went to pay the cleaners, and other similar types of work. One restoration company went so far as to tell Moore he would not be paid, and they didn't care because there were loads of cleaners out there.

After several months of no payments we discovered that Moore was desperate enough to tell the restoration companies that I was out of it, and they should send the checks back to him. They listened to him and two checks were sent to him. We confronted him and he was nervous and apologetic, but admitted he was in bad financial trouble. We discussed the fraud he committed and he agreed to pay me everything he owed.

Today Moore is trying to be honorable. He offered to pay $50 a week until the debt is paid. He has almost

---

[1] Funding invoices to churches can be tricky. First you probably won't be able to find a credit rating. Larger congregations are less risky because they are more likely to be financially stable, and often have a treasurer or bookkeeper on site during the day. Therefore if you need to call about an invoice, you'll be able to find a knowledgeable person available. Small congregations, however, are more likely to be less financially sound, and the bills are usually paid by a volunteer treasurer who writes the checks from home. This person is probably at the church once or twice a week, including Sunday. Just reaching that person to inquire about an overdue invoice (not uncommon) can require the patience of Job.

succeeded in doing that. His debt is about $10,000 at this point.

He knows we won't factor him, but he has at least agreed to work it off.

 Our mistake was not to stay on top of the collection effort effectively. Had we called more often, the restoration company would not have believed Moore that we were out of it. By the time we did follow up, the damage was done.

 We have also learned that the restoration companies, in general, are not an honorable industry (at least not in the territory we were in). Perhaps we could have dug out more information about them before agreeing to fund Moore's business. Also, it is necessary to be more aware of the industry being funded. This dry cleaning shop was in a neighborhood where residents did not do much dry cleaning in general. Business had some very low valleys.

+   +   +

Analysis

This case study illustrates three points quite well. First, we see what an otherwise decent person and honest client will do when faced with a financial crisis: he will act in perceived self-interest.

Knowing it was wrong, Moore instructed customers to redirect payment to him. The rationale is familiar: "I need this more than that factor who has a lot more money than I do." Moore was not a typical crook – he acknowledged what he did and, bless his soul, is paying the debt back. A crook would just disappear. Yet despite his usually honorable way of conducting business, Moore deliberately committed fraud. This is a common development when factoring clients get cornered and don't know what else to do.

While this wasn't the Karps' fault, as they admit they didn't keep close enough contact with his slow payers. That can be very easy to allow, but sharp attention to slow payments is also one of the most important tasks of the factor. Follow-up with slow payments is crucial on-going due diligence. When a payment is later than expected, find out why – and the sooner the better. This makes the customers aware that you're tracking their payments, and they're less likely to pay slowly...or not pay at all, as happened here.

As Rebecca and Jay learned, certain industries – in this case restoration companies – are more known for poor attitudes about paying vendors. When a customer says, as one did, "I'm not paying" even though the invoice was valid and the work completed, there's little you can do short of sending them to collections and hoping the client can make the debt good through recourse. However, such customers frequently have poor credit or no credit listings. Be sure you check out customers' credit *before* buying invoices they are to pay, especially in marginal industries like restoration companies and building contractors.

To his credit, Moore is repaying his $10,000 debt with $50 weekly payments – without the benefit of continued factoring. At that rate, his debt will be paid off in four years. If he has other debts, Moore probably has more reason to go out of business and declare bankruptcy than to tough it out and pay back the debts. Quite frankly, if he pays this in full over that length of time, especially without factoring, the Karps will be very lucky.

13

Goodabee Home Health Staffing

Networking is the way to go. It is often pleasant and can lead to some wonderful opportunities.

We met Addie Column, a QuickBooks trainer, bookkeeper, and web designer at a local Chamber of Commerce meeting. We hit it off, and started to go to some meetings together of various women's organizations. One day, Addie called and said she'd met Hiram Beancounter, an accountant who had a client who needed to factor. That was one big Bing!

We've met with many accountants. Some are enthusiastic and say they think what we do is fascinating and they will keep us in mind. Then some comments or questions make clear they have not grasped how we fund businesses. The inevitable question comes out about how we "lend money." It is difficult enough to get an accountant to understand exactly the kind of funding we do; having them recommend our service to their clients is even more of a challenge. Hiram was more progressive and did not have the "know it all" attitude we often expect from his colleagues.

Hiram made a quick call to Solomon Knowhow of Goodabee Home Health Staffing and arranged a meeting. Sol was a lawyer and wanted to change careers. He was in a large office with several staff handling the growing organization. He was planning to move shortly to smaller quarters to save money as he grew his business.

He explained that he was the businessman of this venture, and had started the operation with a health care specialist. At the same time, Sol was attending college to get a master's degree in health care to be better able to understand the contracts he was negotiating, and to expand his business direction with the proper degree.

In eighteen months, Sol was already becoming so successful he was doubling his business every six months, thus the need for funding. After a brief meeting, Sol clearly understood the concept of factoring and saw its potential impact on his business. He saw he could go out and hire the nurses he needed to perform on new contracts that were sitting on his desk, unsigned at that point.

Goodabee operated by obtaining contracts with various pharmaceutical companies. The pharmaceutical company sold chemotherapy and other invasive drugs prescribed by a doctor. Goodabee hired nurses to administer these drugs in patients' homes, usually taking one to two hours per visit. This specialty had little competition in the area.

Goodabee's problem was paying the growing nursing staff before being paid by the pharmaceutical companies. While these invoices were small, there were many of them. This was not third-party medical funding: even though an insurance company paid the pharmaceutical company, the pharmaceutical paid Goodabee without waiting to receive the insurance payment.

We first attempted to broker this company because of its potential growth. This wasn't really the kind of company we envisioned being in our portfolio. Sol was already working on starting another company which sent specialty nurses around the country to various hospitals to audit tests performed on new drugs before coming to market. This operation had substantially higher dollar invoices, and again, needed nurse specialists who were more highly paid. This seemed out of reach for our small factoring operation at that time. The anticipated growth was large.

Another factoring company, Capital First Incorporated, agreed to fund Goodabee. After a conference call, Sol agreed to the package, although he seemed a bit reluctant. I thought it was the need to pay the discounts, which were actually very good. All the paper work was done, the due diligence completed, and the first batch was prepared.

In a conversation with Capital First, Sol learned that the verification process would include the need to divulge the patients' names as they appeared on the invoices. Sol was very uncomfortable with this and called us in.

As the conversation went on, we discovered the discounts were not what Sol was concerned about. Instead he had reservations about the person he spoke with on the conference call and throughout the due diligence process. Sol was left with the feeling that Capital First was interested in his money only, and nothing beyond that. He was not happy disclosing highly confidential information to a company in which he had little faith.

We admired Sol's sincerity and work ethic and didn't want to see him turned away. Factoring seemed the perfect solution for him and for his growing business. Without factoring he would severely limit his potential. He was already using his credit cards up to their limits and could not see how he could continue. His personal credit was not very good and a very large contract was sitting on his desk. Would he have to turn it down? His operation was organized and smooth running and seemed the perfect candidate for success.

At this point we decided this was a trustworthy individual with whom we would like to work. We told Sol we would handle the process ourselves and provide funding at the same rate quoted by Capital First, although at a slightly lower advance. We figured we could get him started and when he got too big for our company, we'd look for another funding source for him. He immediately agreed, saying he trusted me and would have no trouble turning the names of his patients over to us. And so we began.

Factoring began in May. In December we attended a function to which Sol was invited. He introduced us to the President of the local Chamber of Commerce and stated he was able to grow his business by 130% using our service. This was the very best testimonial, and it was wonderful to be a part of this kind of success.

For a while, early the following year Goodabee gained financial independence and their factoring slowed down to a crawl. They were getting out of debt and began to put away money for payroll, which they started outsourcing. Some additional growing pains ensued and now they are using the funding on an as-needed basis: just what factoring is all about.

There was only about $15,000 outstanding until recently. When these invoices paid off, Goodabee would no longer need our services. Then another growth spurt started and at the current time, there is about $48,000 outstanding. Before this spurt, they had averaged $20,000 per month, with outstandings of $35,000 on average. The structure of the rates was basically set by Capital First. There is a 15 day rate followed by a daily rate thereafter. Although this rate was less than what we usually offered, we agreed to keep it the same. The advance offered by Capital First was 80%. We advance 75%, which Sol accepted.

With all our clients we pay rebates as the receivable is collected. That is, we pay rebates invoice by invoice. We try to pay the rebate as soon as the check is deposited.

Sol's company is the perfect factoring client: he has his own house in order (he is so organized Hiram Beancounter, his accountant, calls for help). Sol understands the benefits of factoring (he immediately grasped the concept, and was excited about the possibilities right from the start) and his customers pay in a timely fashion.

Working with Sol and his company is a pleasure. We realized early on that communication with a prospective client is one of the most important features in accepting a company to factor. If you don't make a good connection, broker them to another funding source. You must enjoy the people in the company because you will be talking with them often.

+   +   +

Analysis

Clients like Sol make factoring a joy. This study shows how a win-win relationship works and the happy results that occur.

This also shows the crucial role played by a client's trust and confidence in the factor. Why did Jaybec end up with this client? Sol found something about Capital First which made him uncomfortable: finances seemed to be their primary interest. This is a fairly common impression larger factors leave on clients, and a big reason small factors are more desirable in many clients' eyes.

Running a small factoring operation with personal service by the principal can, without question, instill confidence in the client. Particularly in a business like Sol's, where confidentiality is vital, clients need to trust their funding source not just with their finances, but with private information about their customers. No trust…no deal.

Diversified Capital Funding

Contact Information
Diversified Capital Funding
Debbi Cook
PO Box 44
Clarkston, MI 48347
Phone: (248) 620-6705
Fax: (248) 620-6245

Debbi Cook

Following high school, Debbi Cook did clerical and bookkeeping work for various companies and temporary services for twelve years until her daughter was born. She then started a day care from her home which she ran for five years. By then she was ready for a change. Debbi happened to learn about factoring and attended the International Factoring Institute and became a Certified Factoring Specialist (CFS) in 1993.

She then brokered clients for two years and during that time encountered several potential clients rejected by larger factors. These factors didn't want to bother with smaller companies. When her first client came with a $3,000 invoice, she decided the time had come to "get her feet wet" and factor this client herself. She bought this first small client's receivables in 1995, and continued to broker larger transactions.

Over time she began buying more accounts and now provides funding for small clients on a full-time basis, brokering only larger deals. Her company prefers to factor clients who begin with a factoring volume approximately $5,000 to $10,000 per month, and will grow with them beyond that.

Debbi is involved in two local Chambers of Commerce, is listed in the International Who's Who of Entrepreneurs, the National Who's Who in Executives and Professionals, and Lexington Who's Who. She participates regularly in the American Cash Flow Association's annual conventions. In her spare time, she enjoys surfing the web and other computer activities, and is always open to new and different adventures.

14

Mary & Gary Wary Screen Printers

This case study shows how factors need to prove themselves to suspicious prospective clients who have learned to be very protective of their business with strangers. This business, owned by a husband and wife named Mary and Gary Wary, were certainly distrustful as we began.

I met Mary at a networking dinner a few months prior to her calling and requesting our services. The first time I went to their place of business to meet them, Gary was very leery of our taking control over their company. He wanted us to have limited contact with their customers. Since their customers knew just the two of them ran their business, they also knew the Warys were too small to have a separate "quality control" department to follow-up with customers. Gary was also leery of our "stealing" their customers and starting our own printing business!

We had our work cut out for us on this one, ensuring the Warys that we were not the least bit interested in starting our own printing business, nor selling their customers' names to their competition! Gary even questioned how he knew he could trust us with the $250 application fee! How did he know we weren't going to leave town with it? Finally able to put their minds at ease, we started slowly and their factoring volume increased as we earned more trust in each other.

We initially contacted some customers to verify invoices, and everything checked out fine. Payments started coming in on time, and everything looked good. Gary still prefers to maintain most of the contact with his customers, although we do call some occasionally for various reasons, but he also really cracks down on them about paying on time.

We've had this account over five years now, and have watched the Warys expand their business each year. We've even helped them move into a building approximately five times their original size. They give us credit for their success! That's a wonderful feeling! And since Gary is the president of the local Chamber of Commerce, he has the opportunity to highly recommend us on a regular basis to the members!

Analysis

The issue of trust again rings loud and clear. Occasionally you run across prospects like this who think you and everyone out there want to do nothing but rip them off. As Debbi wisely did, you must give them some time and space and consistently demonstrate you're honest, dependable, and will do what you say. They need to grasp the fact that *your* business benefits by helping *theirs* do well; you gain nothing by stealing from them. Testimonials from existing clients can help with this.

When people who turn into good clients have important positions in the local Chamber of Commerce or other such organizations, positive spin-offs and referrals can come in droves. Practicing sound business practices, simple honesty, and the Golden Rule will bring in the kind of clients you want with little or no effort and cost. The Warys required a large degree of patience and "walking the talk" on Debbi's part; by providing these she has reaped a great reward.

15

Five-Finger Discount ISP

We were originally approached about factoring Five-Finger Discount ISP by a business associate, Don Tse Nuttin. Don had been factoring this company but was looking to get out of factoring. The owner of Five-Finger, Dewey Snookerem, also happened to be Don's best friend. Dewey was receiving special rates, as well as "confidential" factoring[1] from Don.

As we were still somewhat new, we were willing to "bend some of the rules" in order to jump-start our business. So we agreed to stick with his existing rates which were approximately 1.5 to 2% lower than our average rates for a regular account. This went great for several months. Although Five-Finger had several small invoices which were very tedious and time-consuming to process, we figured factoring this client would help us in the long run.

We then learned the importance of having a lockbox. We allowed payments of factored invoices to be mailed by customers directly to Dewey, who made daily deposits into our bank account since he was right around the corner from our bank. Then he started missing a day or two periodically. Pretty soon, we realized we hadn't received anything in a week. When we called, Dewey said he hadn't received anything, which we found quite odd, but waited it out. Eventually, the payments stopped coming in altogether.

---

[1] "Confidential" or "non-notification" factoring means the client's customers are not informed of the factoring relationship in place. Factors' verifications need to be done more carefully so the customers are not accidentally informed. Occasionally clients will insist on non-notification, but most do not.

Now, there was obviously a problem. Dewey would never return our calls and the secretary, Bea N. Covernbutt, would only say that they didn't have the money. Shortly after this all we could get was voicemail and Bea didn't even work there anymore. Eventually we filed a lawsuit and obtained a judgment against Dewey.

However, Dewey disappeared with no one able to track him down. We drove out to his house, which was vacant. True to form, Don denied knowing his whereabouts. We used a couple collection agencies who claimed to specialize in factoring to try to track him down…but to no avail.

Luckily, we were only out about $5,000 on this one.

+   +   +

Analysis

The lesson here is short and sweet: don't allow clients to receive checks for factored payments, even if it's more convenient. The temptation to "cop" checks, especially if the client is in financial trouble, is far too great. A lockbox, your post office box, or your office address are the only places you should permit for remittances by customers. Giving clients such control over *your* money is just inviting them to take a Five-Finger Discount.

Like Dewey and Bea, most clients who pull this simply vanish. Judgments are worthless if you cannot locate them – which is usually the case.

This is a common pattern for crooks: especially if you are new to the business, they work with you in an honest fashion just long enough to gain your trust and find the cracks in your system. Then they capitalize on your weakness and disappear.

Debbi should have called the customers directly and immediately upon realizing their typical payment pattern had changed. Doing so would have stopped the problem before Dewey had time to disappear. Recovery of all stolen funds is questionable, but he would have taken less. Fortunately, the loss wasn't catastrophic and taught Debbi a very valuable and fundamental factoring practice: when something seems "odd" or out of the ordinary, get to the root of it immediately.

16
Switcheroo
Tool & Die Shop

Switcheroo Tool & Die Shop was referred by a previous customer of another client. The business was owned by a father and son team, the Whiplashes. The father (Snyde) was the owner, and his son (Lee) managed the shop.

While setting up the account we obtained a personal guarantee from both Snyde and Lee, since Lee was running the business and would be signing legal papers also. Unfortunately this precaution did us little good.

Snyde came to us very desperate for money, stating he could increase business by 500% if we could only help him get going. Since we were new to factoring we were very anxious to take on new clients. They had an existing federal tax lien due to their payroll taxes not being paid. We contacted the IRS, and negotiated a deal for them to subordinate their lien if we would pay the IRS a certain percentage from each invoice payment.

Everything was going great at first. Then Switcheroo needed even more money. Of course, we were very hesitant, but agreed to give them minimal reserves, with the remainder going to the IRS. However, we decreased their advance from 70% down to 50%, to allow for the shortfall due to the IRS.

Then the warning signs came. We confirmed with customers the receipt of their product, and the fact that everything "looked ok" before funding. Yet when making collection calls one to two months after parts were delivered, we were informed Switcheroo was providing products with the wrong specs. Because these customers kept extra stock on hand until they needed them, they didn't know of the problem right away. When informed of the problem, Switcheroo agreed to correct the spec issues, but most were left unanswered.

After trying for several months to resolve the defect issues, Switcheroo informed us they were closing their doors because they couldn't afford to keep the business running anymore.

While still following up with their customers (with almost $100,000 in outstanding invoices), we were informed by one of their customers of a new company name. Lee had filed a new company name under his name at a new location, and directed customers to send the payments to the new company! They claimed since it was a new company with a new owner, they had nothing to do with the old company.

However, our attorney said otherwise. Michigan law says that when assets of a company (machinery, equipment, etc.) are transferred, the liabilities are also transferred with it. Although the court ruled in our favor, it was in vain, since Snyde filed bankruptcy right after our judgment, and Lee soon followed suit.

We ended up losing approximately $60,000 actual cash out of pocket, plus any discounts that we would have received – over $100,000.

+   +   +

Analysis

Ouch! Precision-dependent businesses like tool and die shops and machine shops require extra care with verifications to be sure required specs are being met. If they are not, this is the type of problem you can face.

Clients with no integrity like the Whiplashes pull these kinds of tricks (changing names then filing for bankruptcy) to get away with ripping you off. The fault for these problems rest squarely with their shoddy business practices and careless work.

Being new to factoring, Diversified – like most rookies – was eager to get money on the street. However investing $100,000 this quickly indicates a serious over-concentration in one client, especially for a beginning factor. Unfortunately such painful lessons are not unusual among new factors. Therefore you're wise to start factoring very small clients so that lessons like this – which virtually everyone must learn – are not as costly.

JMB Business Funding

Contact Information
JMB Business Funding
Joanne Blaser, President
PO Box 8186
Rockford, IL 61126-8186
Phone: (815) 968-6157
Fax: (815) 968-6174
Email: Busnfund@aol.com
Web Site: www.jmbbusinessfunding.com

Joanne M. Blaser

Before entering the factoring world, Joanne Blaser worked in the telephone industry for 30 years. During that time her experience was very diversified, including long distance and directory assistance, taking orders for new service, changes in service, account billing, accounts payable, and general customer service. She also was responsible for scheduling employees for three offices plus their payroll.

Because of her background she understands many of the problems businesses face, and Joanne takes great pride in the customer service she provides for her factoring clients. She began JMB Business Funding in 1993, acts as a broker most of the time, and has funded a small number of accounts. She became a member of the American Cash Flow Association's Million Dollar Club in 2000.

Joanne is very active in community affairs. Her grandson has been the Illinois state goodwill ambassador (poster child) for the Muscular Dystrophy Association, and

Joanne has been especially active in fundraising for this organization. She is present at the annual Telethon and seeks participants for the annual MDA Great Walk and the U.S. Bank Annual Golf Outing. She donates time raising funds for the Arthritis Foundation as well.

She is a member of her local Chamber of Commerce and involved in several committees including Women Business Owners of the Rockford Area Chamber, the Business Women's Council, the Council of Small Business, and is an Ambassador for the Chamber. She is also a member of the National Federation of Independent Business and several networking groups. She is an active member of the local chapter of Rotary International, as well as in her church.

17

Phussen-Phume Nurse Staffing

I was working hard as a factoring broker, matching clients with the right funding source, when I received a call from a woman named Phyllis Phussen-Phume. Phyllis had started a temp agency staffing CNA's, RN's, and LPN's, mainly to nursing homes. She was also providing home health for the State Department of Rehabilitation. Phyllis had gotten my name from one of the advisors with SCORE (Service Corps of Retired Executives).

When I had all the preliminary information gathered, I called a couple of factoring companies and was turned down. The reasons were either because of the small size of the transactions, the type of staffing being done involved third party insurance payments, or payments involved the medical industry.

I really wanted to help Phyllis and since I was about to receive an influx of cash from an inheritance, I decided I would jump in and factor my first client. I typed the contracts, had them signed, filed the UCC, and was now in the factoring business.

Phyllis had no computer or billing system, and since I was upgrading my computer system I sold her my two used computers and printer. Not having the cash to pay me, we rolled the transfer of equipment into a loan which she was to pay back out of rebates from her factoring.

For a couple of years, things went very well. Phyllis' business grew. She even opened another office in Arizona. As the business blossomed so did our friendship.

The Arizona company obviously needed financing so I agreed to fund this company as well. Now I was factoring two companies for the same client. This company grew substantially and I realized I wasn't financially able to factor both of them. At this point I referred Phyllis to another factor for the Arizona company. I thought it would be best to fund the company that was in my area so I could keep a better handle on what was happening here.

 After working with her for two years, I learned she had been remiss in maintaining proper state licenses. Phyllis was forced to stop staffing for a period of time while proper paperwork was put into place. By the time she was up and running again, several of her previous clients had found other agencies. Also, because of cost considerations, nursing homes were avoiding staffing agencies and were using their own employees.

Since this part of Phyllis' customer base had pretty much dried up, she decided to become Medicare certified and focus on getting referrals from clinics and hospitals for home health patients.

During this time, her income drastically dropped and she needed money, so she asked me if I would give her a loan. Since I had worked with her so long (three years) and since I really considered her a friend, I loaned her money. BAD MOVE! This new debt was added to what she still owed on the computers. The earlier debt remained because most of the time she needed all the money due from rebates which were supposed to pay her debt for the computers. Trying to be helpful, I didn't always insist on receiving the monthly payments I was owed. BAD MOVE! Her debt to me was growing deeper.

Phyllis was still doing minimal work for the state, when all of a sudden the state stopped sending the payments, holding the money for taxes owed. I had been asking her all along if she had been keeping her taxes current, and was assured that she was, but found out this was not true. So now the debt increased from these tax withholdings.

To add to the problem, one of the nursing homes she had been staffing filed bankruptcy, and because of our recourse agreement she owed me for the unpaid advances and discounts of this bankrupt customer. The hole kept getting deeper; at this point she owed me for the computers, the cash loan, the charged back advances and discounts from the tax withholdings, and now chargebacks for the bankrupt customer.

Believe it or not, things got worse. By this time Medicare was starting to pick up. I told her I wasn't really comfortable funding Medicare payments because I didn't understand how they worked…and she didn't either. I was told that Medicare wouldn't send the checks to any address except the vendor, and since we had had an excellent working relationship, I agreed that if she would notify me when the payments arrived and give them to me, I would go along with the program. BAD MOVE!!

Against my better judgment, I agreed to advance on the Medicare clients. I learned about Medicare real fast, and what I learned is this: Medicare payments are unbelievably complicated.

a) For each case an "episode" dollar amount is given.
b) Each episode is for 60 days. Two payments are received from Medicare per episode. The first payment is 60% of the episode amount, and the second payment at the end of the 60 days is for the balance.
c) Billing is submitted electronically by a medical billing company.

Now, how should I structure advances and rebates for payments like this? For the first payment of an episode I advanced Phyllis 70% of the 60% payment. Then for the end of the episode, I would give 70% of the remaining 40%.

If a patient is new, Medicare pays 60% of the episode amount after billing has been electronically submitted. The first payment (called the RAP) is usually within 3 weeks. Since Phyllis was always in need of funds, she wanted the rebates as soon as payments came in, and I accommodated her. Unfortunately I did not realize that Medicare payments can be "taken back." That is, if there is a discrepancy of the RAP (if they need more information), Medicare will pull back the first payment by taking it from the next remittance for another patient episode due the vendor. They may also take the RAP back if the end of the claim is not filed in a manner they consider "timely." This late filing happened on three occasions and other "take backs" happened multiple times.

Moreover, Phyllis needed the advance on the second portion of the episode which I gave her when the RAP payment arrived. Often this was several weeks before final billing occurred. I had been under the impression that the last payment would be made immediately upon the date of the end of the episode. I think Phyllis had the same impression because she didn't seem to know that she had to close the case with documentation to receive the second payment. When I realized this, I told her that I couldn't advance on the end of the episode until the ending date.

At the end of the episode the claim is submitted with necessary documentation, and that payment comes usually four to six weeks after the final billing is received. If the final billing isn't sent within a certain time frame they will take back the RAP (first payment) from whatever account is next in line to be paid.

When Medicare sends the final remittance, they show a payment of the entire episode amount, with a take back amount of the original 60% payment. At first it was very confusing, because there seemed to be minuses everywhere. If the RAP payment was being made, only the starting episode date was shown. If the end of episode (EOE) payment was being made, it showed the beginning *and* the ending dates.

Are you ready for more government process? If the patient is recertified for another 60 days, Medicare pays 50% of the episode amount (RAP) instead of 60%, again within three weeks, and the last 50% at the end of the certification (EOE). That was also not clear until we received the first payment and it was for 50% instead of 60%. The rebate had already been paid, so now I was short. Again. That meant Phyllis owed me still more, this time for short payments.

To make matters worse Phyllis wasn't getting referrals as fast as she had hoped, and was again in need of advances with no completed invoices. Remember, each claim was for 60 days; for example January 9 to March 9. The first advance would be made on about January 20 after the patient was seen for the minimum visits required. Then on March 9 (EOE) the last advance would be made on the 40% EOE.

Problem: by the middle of the second month (February), Phyllis was in dire need of funds but the case could not be final billed until March 9. I tried to explain to her that if I gave her an advance on the last 40% (three weeks before she could send the final paperwork), when March 9 came around she would be unable to make payroll. Her answer was that she was the nurse on many of the cases and she could wait to be paid.

So again, against my better judgment, I advanced before billing was completed. BAD MOVE!! Since Phyllis was calling me each time a payment came in, and she was giving me the checks to apply to advances, I thought this would be okay.

About this time, I was leaving town for a week. The day I was to leave Phyllis called and faxed over some billings and said she needed an advance before I left. Again, I went out of my way and made sure money was transferred into her bank account.

When I came back to my office, I tried to contact her but my calls were never returned. When I finally was able to reach her, I found out she had received checks for some patients and had cashed and kept the payments. Her excuse: I wasn't giving her rebates that were due. When I questioned her about which rebates she was referring to, she told me of two payments she had given me (which she hadn't), so I assumed the checks had been lost.

I called Medicare to check on what had happened to the payments and was told that the checks had been cashed. I asked for a copy and found that Phyllis had cashed them. When I confronted her, she denied doing so until I was able to show her that she had, indeed, cashed the checks. In fact, she had kept and cashed a total of five checks.

The very next thing I did was go to the post office and change the mailing address to mine, since this was allowed in our agreement. Then I called my attorney who suggested I go to her office and repossess the computers, which I tried to do with my husband's help. I had all of my legal agreements with me, so when she wanted to call the police, I let her do so.

When the police officer arrived he listened to our story and read my agreements, but sided with her saying it was a civil matter and I couldn't just walk in and take equipment. So we left and called the attorney. He said if we had called him from Phyllis' office, he would have advised just to leave with the computers because once off the property there would have been nothing she could have done.

At this point, I set up an appointment with my attorney. I brought all of the documentation I had and as he was reading through the agreements, he found a glitch which referred to where the trial would be held if necessary. I had used the Accounts Receivable Purchase Agreement of an out of state factor, which listed the trial venue as Washington state. Because of this error, we would have to rely only on the Personal Guarantee and the UCC-1. Suggestion: READ AND REREAD all your documents making sure all t's are crossed and i's dotted...and that *your* state and county are the place of venue.

Several days passed and only one piece of mail was redirected to my office. Then Phyllis called and asked if I were getting her mail. When she found out the mail had been redirected she called the post office, whose legal department called me. They asked for copies of the legal documents, which I faxed, and sent the hard copy. They agreed to hold the mail for us to pick up with a third party present.

Phyllis made a big scene the day we went to pick up the mail because she didn't want the third party to take the mail. We tried explaining that the third party wasn't going to keep the mail, only pass it on to us. When she finally agreed, the person at the post office said they wouldn't give us the mail that day and we would have to come back when a supervisor was present.

Because of the scene she had made, the supervisor of the postal sub-station didn't want us to come there to pick up the mail and insisted that we have the mail directed to a post office box at the main post office. We could pick up the mail only with the third party and both of us present. This worked for a while, but no checks were received. Why? Medicare checks cannot be forwarded to a temporary address, so the checks were being returned to Medicare.

I tried to resolve the situation by talking with the supervisor at the postal substation to see if they would hold the mail for us to pick up there together. At first the answer was no, but he told me to call the customer relations manager. The reason the post office was hesitant to work with us is because of the scenes Phyllis Phussun-Phume made, both in the facility and over the phone. Since I was much calmer they were willing to listen to me and agreed to let us pick up the mail – together, until I had been paid – provided Phyllis could behave herself. Now, each time we go in, if the clerk doesn't know us both we are required to show ID (which is a good situation as far as I am concerned).

My attorney sent a letter to Medicare indicating that I was the irrevocable assignee for her accounts and that all payments were required to be sent to me. The letter further stated that any funds sent to Phyllis would not constitute payment of her invoices, but thus far the payments are still being sent to Phyllis. Nonetheless, the only way she can receive the mail is for me to be with her.

However, another problem has arisen. Medicare has started EFT (electronic funds transfer) payments directly to her account. I found this out when a remittance came in the mail with no check attached. Medicare can't seem to be uniform with the process, because we are still getting some checks by mail. Phyllis has agreed to tell me when funds are transferred via EFT, and I will ultimately know because the explanation remittance always comes by mail.

I am slowly being repaid. Realizing that Phyllis needs money to keep her business afloat, I don't keep the entire amount of the payments, even when the entire check should go towards invoices I have factored. I've explained to her that what she has done is fraud and that another factoring company wouldn't be as lenient as I. Further, if she doesn't work with me I can have her arrested. So far this is working.

+   +   +

Analysis

Whew! What a case study! In case you were wondering, this is the case study that inspired this book.

After reading this and seeing what Joanne has been through with both Phyllis and Medicare, I absolutely cannot comprehend why any small factor familiar with this case study would accept Medicare payments. This case shows why I so strongly recommend not factoring third party medical receivables in general, and Medicare/Medicaid payments in particular.

The other risks in this case can be traced back to ignorance. Neither Phyllis nor Joanne knew Medicare procedures and this lack of knowledge came to haunt them.

Further, Phyllis dug an early hole for herself by using her rebates to pay off the loan for the computers. As we saw with Need It Now Manufacturing in Case Study 10, a factor who provides a loan in the first place then allows the loan to be paid off with future rebates is playing with fire. With Phyllis, other events deepened her debt making the factoring relationship quite messy. As I've said many times, "Do not give loans to clients." Buy their invoices, but do not loan them money. Period. This case study is a classic example of the complications that can result from making loans which too often cannot be repaid.

Notice the number of times Joanne says, "…against my better judgment." Listening to and following your common sense is so important! Heed that inner voice. To her credit, Joanne always acted generously toward Phyllis and provided advances and rebates time after time to bail Phyllis out of a problem. However, a few factors will be nice all the way to the poor house. There comes a time when saying "No" is more prudent and better in the long run than being kind.

While most factors would simply pull the plug and let Phyllis' business die, thereafter reclaiming what they can in bankruptcy court, Joanne has hung in there and continued to help Phyllis. Unfortunately for Joanne, her kindness has led to a debt that Phyllis will probably not be able to completely repay.

Few factors would have stuck with Phyllis the way Joanne has. Sadly, Phyllis now views Joanne as "the bad guy" for trying to collect funds that are legitimately due Joanne, after Phyllis fraudulently banked the checks. This will not incline Phyllis to want to repay or cooperate with Joanne, which does not bode well for Joanne's full repayment.

As we've seen before, when funding any kind of temp agency, factors are wise to require the client to use a payroll service. The factors must receive regular reports to certify the taxes are paid correctly and on time. This leads to another reason Joanne's chances of full repayment are slim. Not mentioned in the details of this case study is the fact that in addition to the $17,000 Phyllis owes Joanne, Phyllis also owes the IRS over $100,000 for unpaid payroll taxes.

KLT&J, Inc.

Contact Information
KLT & J Inc.
Ken Earnhardt
Mailing
PMB 171
1000 Johnnie Dodds Blvd. #103
Mt. Pleasant, SC 29464
Phone: (843) 971-3883
Toll Free: (877) 971-3883
Fax: (843) 856-3927
Email: customerservice@kltjfactoring.com
Web Site: www.kltjfactoring.com

Ken Earnhardt

KLT&J, Inc. is a family-owned factoring business run by Ken Earnhardt. His experience with factoring goes back to the late 1970's when he and his wife LaNell owned a small textile recycling company. They were approached by a factoring company out of Greenville, South Carolina about their cash flow needs. Since they did have cash flow issues, Ken and LaNell immediately signed up for the service.

The Earnhardts were the factor's second client (Ken's father was the first). That particular factoring company is still in operation today. Because of this first-hand experience of being a factoring client, Ken has an insight into the issues that a small company faces and are well-equipped to address their needs.

In the early 1980's Ken were contacted by a young lady from church about managing her money while she was on the mission field in Honduras for two years. He felt an awesome responsibility to insure that she gain as much as possible on her money for that period. Not understanding the stock market, bonds, or mutual funds very well, Ken decided to use her money to factor some of his company's receivables.

He knew his business and was comfortable with factoring some of his accounts since he was still factoring with the company in Greenville. Little did he know that some fifteen years later a part-time business would turn into a full time career! What's more, that young lady is still an investor today.

Ken founded KLT&J, Inc. for the purpose of funding small companies who cannot qualify for financing. The business not only enables these companies to continue to grow, it also provides a place where small investors can put their money and get a decent return. That philosophy has served well over the years. The services they offer are:

- Factoring
- Accounts Receivable Management
- Business Incubator Program
- Counseling

18

Greener Grass Landscaping

This case study shows the importance of knowing your client. A young man named Digger Busch was referred to me by one of my clients for counseling. In our initial meeting he told me of his desire to leave his present job as manager of a well-known restaurant. His desire was to go into the landscaping business full time. I told him that I would need to meet with both him and his wife before I could give him further direction.

The next meeting involved a discussion with his wife, Karen Boutbilz, regarding how she felt about Digger leaving his current job. Needless to say she was terrified and I helped relieve some of her anxiety when I told her that if he would do as I counseled everything would work out smoothly. Of course Karen's biggest concern was with the family finances. I asked if they would be willing to reduce their debt and live on a budget until such time that their finances were in order. They both agreed – Digger thought they would be able to clear the way to start the business within a couple of months. (I knew better!)

The next meeting involved them both taking a personality profile so that they would have a better understanding of each other, their fears, and their abilities. Anyone who goes into business without the full support and understanding of his spouse is setting himself up for failure – if not in the business, then in the marriage! Digger and Karen both decided they wanted to enter our Business Incubator Program when the time was right.

It took seven months for the time to be right and for their finances to be in order so I could recommend he quit his job and go into business. In our Business Incubator program, we will lease equipment and manage all aspects of the business including bookkeeping, invoicing, banking, and collections. This frees the business owner to be able to just go out and do the work and grow his business.

I had monthly meetings with Digger to go over the numbers with him and to educate him in how to manage the business. Little by little different aspects are turned over to the client as they grow and are able to hire people to do the bookkeeping, invoicing, etc.

Digger left his job at the restaurant in May and by the end of that year his new business, Greener Grass Landscaping, had done a total of over $100,000 in business. It is easy to grow a business if you have the right kind of help and can concentrate on getting customers. He continues to grow and is well on his way to doing $250,000 in business by year end.

+   +   +

Analysis

As this case study illustrates, small factors frequently work with people who have zero experience owning and running a business. Unless they receive (and accept) the financial guidance and business suggestions a factor can often provide, mistakes are common. This helps explain why such a large percentage of start up companies fail: they are undercapitalized and the owner has no clue how to run a business successfully. Like Digger, they underestimate expenses, overestimate income, and are naïve about time lines.

Large factors, because they work with larger clients, don't usually deal with people like Digger. They not only require larger invoice volume, but quite frankly, they prefer to work with more sophisticated business owners. People like Digger require a lot of "hand-holding" which translates into a lot of time. Time is money to large factors, so they just don't want clients like this who will require a lot of time and provide little if any profit. And because there are so many Diggers out there, the need for small factors is enormous.

Most larger factors are more than happy to let someone else work with them.

Small factors like KLT&J, who make a point of providing the help such people so badly need, are doing a tremendous favor to both the client whose business they incubate, and the larger factors who will fund that business once it is beyond its infancy. When small factors recognize the value their services provide, they appreciate what a crucial need they fill…and clients like Digger appreciate it, too. Just ask them.

19

Just Trust Me Map Makers

This case study is about trusting your gut instincts. In my zeal to grow my factoring business I went against a "bad feeling" I had about a potential client, Sylvester (Sly) Foxgleam of Just Trust Me Map Makers. Sly's business involved producing and distributing local area maps. I came into the picture because he wanted to factor the advertising sales that were placed on the maps.

Sly found us on the internet through a matchmaking web site which matches businesses seeking capital with funders seeking clients.

Warning Number 1 (which I ignored). In my initial conversation I asked Sly if he had been contacted by other factors since he posted his request on the matchmaking website. He said that he had but he wanted to use someone who was small and more local (Sly was in a neighboring state). He said, "I can tell just by talking to you that you are the kind of person I want to deal with, because you sound trustworthy *just as I'm trustworthy."* Lesson: I am now very leery of anyone who tells me how trustworthy he is.

Warning Number 2 (which I ignored). I decided to go ahead and have him complete the application process. It was like pulling teeth to get all the information that was required. Sly never gave me complete information without my requesting it numerous times and he wanted to have me deduct the application fee ($250) from his first factoring. Lesson: If a client won't pay the application fee (if you charge one) and won't give you complete and accurate information, then he will not factor complete and accurate invoices and will not pay you when accounts go into default.

Warning Number 3 (which I ignored). It is my practice to meet personally with all my clients before I begin factoring their accounts so I arranged to meet this man at the address that was on his application. When I called to confirm our meeting he asked if we could meet at his home instead. Although I had a feeling that something wasn't right, I agreed.

When I arrived he was very cordial and we had lunch at his table and he proceeded to tell me how his business worked and who his major customers were. Needless to say, I was convinced this man had a legitimate business. Lesson: Verify the address of the business and insist on meeting at that address. If they say that they can't meet at that address

then postpone the meeting until they can or drop them as a potential client.

Our relationship was off and running and he was factoring about $7,000 per month. As time went by we began to get calls and letters from some of his customers complaining that they were receiving invoices from us for services that he had not rendered. We ceased funding him immediately and began to try to collect from him on these accounts. He resisted and is now in the hands of an attorney. Our exposure: $7,000.

+   +   +

Analysis

This case study repeats a familiar pattern from other negative factoring experiences:

1) The factor has a vague but uneasy feeling about a client.

2) The client somehow instills enough confidence in the factor's mind to persuade the factor to release funds.

3) Funds are advanced despite the factor's misgivings.

4) The client starts off fine but problems arise little by little. In this case, invoices were created for services not rendered.

5) When follow-up efforts are initiated by the factor to recoup funds, the client resists or simply disappears.

6) The factor hands the account to legal or collection professionals, and prepares to write the loss off to bad debt.

The purpose of verifying invoices – especially if you have reservations about a client – is evident here. In reality, though, verifying every single invoice of every single client is practically impossible. What's more, even thorough verifications can be thwarted by collusion between a client and his customer.

Thus we return full-circle to following your instincts, and setting and keeping limits on clients. By setting and maintaining credit limits, avoiding over-concentrations, and living within your self-imposed guidelines, you limit the loss you can experience. Luckily for Ken the amount he stands to lose with Sly is not devastating.

20

Smoldering Embers Advertising Resources Unltd.

Smoldering Embers Advertising Resources Unltd. (SEARU) was owned and operated by Corey Rotten. SEARU produced ads for radio and television commercials and was referred to us by another client.

This case study occurred during our first year as a full time factor and is about questioning explosive growth of your client. Here again, because we had money that we wanted to "get on the street," we were caught up in the excitement of the growth of a client who had been with us for about six months. Here are the events as they unfolded.

First, Corey had a large increase in the number of invoices he was factoring. He explained he was very pleased that factoring had allowed him to grow so quickly. The next event was a significant increase in the invoice values he was factoring. Corey told us he was anticipating growth of about 25% per month. However just a couple days later he called and said that the growth would be around 40% instead. He began using current factoring to pay off old invoices (this is a bad sign!)

At this point we had close to $500,000 in receivables to SEARU. We did not have enough capital to fund the kind of growth Corey was expecting so we told him we could not handle his account any more, but we would turn him over to another factor who would be able to meet his needs going forward. His response was that if we could not fund him he would just stop factoring all together. Corey said that since we were not funding him any more his cash flow would be greatly diminished and he would only be able to pay us about $60,000 per month until the account was paid in full.

This was definitely a red flag since we had assumed the invoices we had funded were legitimate and that those customers would be paying us. We asked for the phone numbers for each of the customers and were given the run around. We collected payments from SEARU for about six months until their office and records were destroyed by fire. At this point we were owed a little over $200,000.

We were given a document (phony) that indicated SEARU had accounts payable insurance and that we would be paid by the insurance company. We were relieved to think that we would come out of this situation without a loss. However, there was a long investigation into the cause of the fire. We finally had to sue and settle for a payment of $70,000. Our total loss: $132,000.

Lesson: When clients add a large number of new customers…verify, verify, verify. When average invoice values increase…verify, verify, verify.

+   +   +

Analysis

The price of rookie mistakes again rears its head.

As Ken indicates in his last paragraph, his verification process was inadequate or simply nonexistent with SEARU. When a factor is new to the business and any time a client is new, invoice verifications are a very important part of standard and ongoing due diligence. KLT&J made an often committed error common to honest, decent people who take for granted the honesty and decency of their new clients: "we had *assumed* the invoices we had funded were legitimate and that those customers would be paying us."

When a dishonest client sees you're never checking the validity of his invoices, he may consider this "carte blanche" to take advantage of you. Corey did this to the tune of half a million dollars.

When Ken said he would need to refer Corey to a larger factor and Corey refused, this was a good indication that

Corey feared being caught in his game by a larger, more experienced factor. If he had been honest and his growth was real, he would have welcomed the added cash once he realized he had outgrown KLT&J's ability to fund. Refusing this referral was a huge red flag.

Even when beginning factors have a sizeable pool of funds, having $500,000 out with one client is an extremely dangerous over-concentration in that client. When you're starting out, fund very small businesses (I recommend under $10,000 per month to start, as with Freddy Reddy's Steady Carpet Cleaning in Case Study 1). Limit your exposure by establishing low credit limits to start. Save your funds for the future when your procedures are refined and you've learned valuable lessons from early mistakes.

KLT&J was fortunate such a large hit so early in their factoring experience didn't completely kill their business. For many beginning small factors, a loss of $132,000 would end their factoring careers in a heartbeat.

21

Gofer Gold Traveling Nurses Service

This case study is what makes being a small factor so fulfilling.

Many banks, lending institutions, and even some factors do not like to fund a start-up. Seymour Horizon, one of two owners of Gofer Gold Traveling Nurses Service, came to us months before he even opened his doors for business so he would have funding in place to fuel his growth. He was referred by our account manager at American Express Financial Services, who attended the same church as Seymour. His company placed "traveling nurses" in various hospitals throughout the country. The nurses' assignments were usually for 3 to 6 months.

Because Seymour was already set up to fund his receivables he was very confident about placing nurses as quickly as he could recruit them. Within twelve months he was factoring an average of $125,000 every two weeks.

One thing I had learned in the past was to avoid client concentration. Gofer Gold was becoming a larger and larger portion of our portfolio and although the relationship was perfect we decided that we could not keep up with their growth. Unknown to us at the time, Gofer Gold was being courted by a large factor specializing in this industry. We encouraged Seymour to make the change. This year Gofer Gold Traveling Nurses Service will do volume of over $6,000,000.

Meanwhile, Seymour and the other owner have parted ways. Seymour has again come to us to set up factoring for his *new* traveling nurse business. The lesson: never burn your bridges even if you lose a client. You never know what the future holds!

+   +   +

Analysis

Short and sweet! Here's an honest, forward-looking client who saw the value of factoring before opening his doors. Having factoring in place once he was ready to roll, Seymour never once experienced cash flow shortfalls so common to most new and young companies. He enjoyed steady and manageable growth and had funding in place to enable him to look for and accept new customers. What a great example of a proactive, rather than reactive, business owner!

As Gofer Gold outgrew the resources of KLT&J, a larger factor was ready and eager to accept this highly desirable account. This illustrates how small factors help not only very small and young businesses, they incubate them for larger factors who are usually glad to accept clients who have been managed properly by a good small factor. And as Ken wisely suggests, never burn your bridges with a good client! Providing excellent service and good relationships can pay off even after you think your service is no longer needed. Satisfied clients not only refer others to you, they return when circumstances change and they need you again.

Conclusion

As we conclude *Factoring Case Studies* and review the mix of good and bad experiences, these general observations can be made.

Factors' Vulnerability

Factors are especially vulnerable to loss and fraud when they are new to the business. Without the benefit of experience, they are less able to recognize risk and are an easier mark for dishonest people. Of the eleven negative case studies described, five – nearly half – occurred when the factors were new or recently under way in their factoring careers.

On the other hand, the fact that the remaining half of the bad experiences happened when the factors were more experienced is good reason to continue to maintain low exposures, never to let your guard down, and never to assume your procedures make you invincible. Factoring involves risk; therefore you must follow specific strategies to minimize your risk at all times.

While there are a very small number of individuals who intentionally set you up to cheat you (Izzy Real in Case Study 8), others commit acts of fraud when a tempting opportunity presents itself. This usually occurs when the factor exhibits somewhat careless procedures (Dewey Snookerem in Case Study 15, and Corey Rotten in Case Study 20). Even more commonly, when the client is backed into a corner and sees no other way out (David D. Shiner in Case Study 3, Moore N. Need in Case Study 12, and Phyllis Phussen-Phume in Case Study 17), he will justify his dishonesty with the rationalization that he needs the money more than the wealthy factor.

Other factoring losses result from clients who simply have no integrity (I.M. Hy, Case Study 7, and Snyde and Lee Whiplash, Case Study 16). These people selfishly act in their own best interest despite the harm it causes the factor who has helped them. Still other clients are extremely poor managers and unaware of regulations or practices that impact their businesses (Phyllis Phussen-Phume, Case Study 17). As you can see, the factoring landscape is littered with land mines and risks lurk under many innocent-looking stones.

Factors' Mistakes

Factoring Small Receivables (Book 2 of *The Small Factor Series*) contains a chapter entitled "Common Mistakes." This chapter lists nineteen errors often made by both new and experienced small factors. Of these nineteen, eleven are clearly evident here in *Factoring Case Studies*. Further, *Factoring Fundamentals* (Book 1 of *The Small Factor Series)* suggests six industries or types of receivables small factors are wise to avoid. Three of these were funded (to the factors' regret) in these case studies.

Below is a list of these eleven mistakes made and the three industries unfortunately funded, and the Case Studies in which these are exhibited.

Mistake	Case Studies	
Inadequate Due Diligence	3	We Always eXpect More Floors
	4	Slippery Cliff International Press
	8	NoGoodnicks.com
	16	Switcheroo Tool & Die Shop
	19	Just Trust Me Map Makers
	20	SEARU
Not Saying "No"	8	NoGoodnicks.com
	10	Need It Now Manufacturing
	17	Phussen-Phume Nurse Staffing
Advancing Too Much	8	NoGoodnicks.com
	20	SEARU

Risk Minimization Strategies

Factoring Fundamentals discusses four general strategies for minimizing risk. To some degree they are the antithesis of the mistakes mentioned above. The strategies and their sub-points are:

1) Set Financial Limits
2) Determine Receivables You Will and Will Not Factor
3) Perform Adequate Due Diligence
   a) Client Due Diligence
   b) Customer Due Diligence
   c) New Invoice Due Diligence
   d) Overdue Invoice Due Diligence
4) Establish and Build Up Reserves

This book has been filled with examples which put these strategies into practice, particularly numbers 1 and 3. When these strategies were not practiced, problems frequently resulted.

Several case studies point to the value of performing proper due diligence, particularly strategy 3c. Verify invoices to make sure the product or service has been received and payment will be made to the factor's address. Many of the bad experiences resulted because the factors neglected these verifications.

We've seen the numerous risks that go with factoring – dishonest, selfish, careless, and otherwise untrustworthy clients and customers, and errors in procedures or judgment made by many factors. Therefore common sense suggests a factor's foremost strategy is to set financial limits, thereby putting minimal amounts at risk. This is especially prudent when the factor is new, even if his or her pool of factoring funds is sizeable.

Kari and Kevin Clark of Premier Funding started us off well in Case Study 1, factoring Fred Reddy, a small carpet cleaning company. Fred's monthly factoring volume never exceeded $10,000. Even if the Clarks had experienced a loss with Fred (which they never did), such a set back would not have been insurmountable. Losses such as $115,000 with

David D. Shiner in Case Study 3, or $132,000 with Corey Rotten in Case Study 20 would cripple if not wipe out most new small factors. I have long recommended small "Mom and Pop" carpet cleaners and janitorial companies factoring around $5,000 per month as ideal clients for new factors. The Clarks illustrate the results of this advice superbly.

The most important risk minimization strategy is to avoid over-concentration. Following normal due diligence and standard factoring practices will lessen the chance of fraud, loss from client errors, loss from mistakes by the factor, and so on. But your greatest weapon for avoiding a catastrophic loss is a simple, cost-free procedure: set credit limits with clients and customers, and limit the size of invoices you buy. Then *stay within these limits and do not make exceptions.* If you increase a client's credit limit, do so in relatively small increments only after clients have proven to be honest and customers payments have proven to be dependable.

Further, set an absolute ceiling which no client's credit limit will exceed. If a client outgrows this limit, broker him to a larger factor or participate as a co-factor, and continue to earn commissions. Two contributors did this successfully: Richard Shapiro with Happy Helping Hands Temporary Agency (Case Study 9), and Ken and LaNell Earnhardt with Gofer Gold Traveling Nurses Service (Case Study 21).[1]

While using this strategy will not prevent losses, you will avoid catastrophic events fatal to your business. This is the simplest yet most often overlooked (or ignored) risk management tool that any factor can employ. The reason? I'm not sure, but my guess is greed has taken at least temporary control of the factor's thinking.

---

[1] Notice that both of these involved temp agencies. Such growth is a common occurrence in this industry, so don't be too disappointed when such clients outgrow your small factoring operation. Be ready to refer them to a larger factor when the time comes.

The Core of Factoring: People

When all the risks are taken into account and protective measures are in place, we come back to the human element at the core of factoring. Factors deal with finances and business procedures, but everything comes down to human interactions. These relations involve reciprocal trust and working together for mutual benefit. When these positive attributes are in place and potential hazards overcome, the practice of factoring works. The results are financially quite rewarding and emotionally very satisfying.

Consider the successful case studies we've seen:

- Fred Reddy and the Clarks, who improved Fred's bookkeeping system and have enjoyed a steady and mutually profitable factoring relationship for over four years.

- Jeeves and Holly Goodfellow who received funding of over $400,000 in nine months with Mach 1 Funding. The overwhelming majority of their payments are received in 30 days, and both factor and client have benefited handsomely from working together.

- "MagicAl" Gonn who, despite having no funds of his own, realized a net profit of $15,000 in just two months with Mach 1's financial assistance and the expertise of Phil Hazpull, a garment industry specialist.

- The creative role Richard Shapiro played with Lack of Moolah Construction Suppliers. Richard's skills led to a happy ending for his client, a contractor, a developer, and a home owner – when it looked like years of court battles were inevitable.

- The business-saving assistance Richard's company, Condor International Financial Services, provided Happy Helping Hands Temporary Agency when a large factor's self-serving pullout over a payroll error brought them to the brink of disaster.

- Sharon Truegrit, who in spite of financial difficulties, repaid Jaybec Business Funding for losses caused by dishonest customers through no fault of her own.

- Solomon Knowhow of Goodabee Home Health Staffing who trusted Jay and Rebecca Karp with confidential information, when he felt uncomfortable sharing patients' names with a larger factor. This trust has led to a mutually satisfying and beneficial relationship.

- The patience and trustworthiness Debbi Cook showed Gary Wary, the screen printer who was distrustful of everyone at first. Now five years later, Gary has been her best client and his influence as President in the Chamber of Commerce has provided numerous recommendations for Debbi's business.

- Digger Busch who realized his dream of running his own landscaping business, made possible by the wise counsel of Ken Earnhardt and factoring funds from KLT&J, Inc.

- Seymour Horizon who had the foresight to arrange factoring with KLT&J even before he opened his traveling nurses business. Thanks to his prudent moves and ever-available cash with factoring, his company has outgrown KLT&J's services and this year will do a volume of over $6 million. And when Seymour and his partner parted, he returned to KLT&J to fund his new business.

Yes, factoring can be risky. Factoring can also be extremely rewarding when you work with good people, know you are providing a much-needed service, follow sound business practices, and make a very high return on investment.

As these case studies have shown, factoring is an intensely people-centered business. Factoring certainly involves business financing, but it is far more than that. Factoring is relationships. Factoring requires trust while demanding street smarts. Factoring requires common sense.

Factoring brings out the very best and the very worst in people.

If you are highly risk-averse, factoring is not for you. If you are motivated solely by profit, you will not be a good factor, you will neither deserve nor earn your clients' loyalty, and you will not enjoy the people with whom you work. If you go into factoring only to help people, your good intentions will get clobbered and your sense of innocence shredded.

Those who lack the right perspective or are careless don't stay in factoring. We read of two instances (Case Studies 10 and 15) where factors were leaving the business. You'll learn of others who drop out as you spend time in this field.

However, factors who run their operations properly, show sound judgment, use common sense, make excellent income, and help many businesses, tend to stick around. These are the people who enjoy the rewards of factoring for a very long time. If you factor with a realistic approach, a cautious attitude, and a desire to improve your clients' lives as well as your own, you will find factoring a fascinating and highly rewarding business.

Appendix

The Small Factor Series

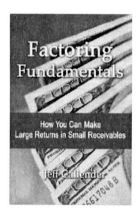

Book 1
*Factoring
Fundamentals*

Book 2
*Factoring
Small Receivables*

Book 3
*Factoring
Case Studies*

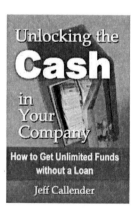

Book 4
*Unlocking the Cash
in Your Company*

About this Series

The Small Factor Series is designed to:

1. Introduce readers to the investment of factoring small business receivables.

2. Provide a step-by-step manual with complete instructions for small factors.

3. Provide numerous real-life examples of factoring clients from the files of people who have been investing in small receivables for some time

4. Introduce factoring to small business owners and provide answers to numerous questions these potential factoring clients have.

Each book in the series is written to address the above points:

- Book 1, *Factoring Fundamentals: How You Can Make Large Returns in Small Receivables,* provides the introduction.

- Book 2, *Factoring Small Receivables: How to Make Money in Little Deals the Big Guys Brush Off,* is the step-by-step manual.

- Book 3, *Factoring Case Studies: Learn and Profit from Experienced Small Factors,* describes real client experiences of small factors which illustrate the many lessons and suggestions made in the first two volumes.

- Book 4, *Unlocking the Cash in Your Company: How to Get Unlimited Funds without a Loan,* introduces small business owners to factoring and how it can help their cash flow

All are available from www.DashPointPublishing.com.

Other Books by Jeff Callender

 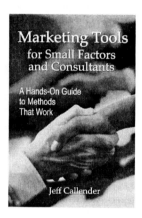

Factoring Wisdom

Marketing Tools for Small Factors and Consultants

Scores of factoring topics are succinctly discussed in **Factoring Wisdom,** a collection of short quotes from *The Small Factor Series* and *FactorTips.* Grouped alphabetically by subject, this little volume provides a thumbnail sketch of the Jeff Callender's writings. This digest is an excellent and inexpensive way for the newcomer to enter the world of factoring, as well as an easy yet thorough review of prominent subjects in the series.

Marketing Tools for Small Factors and Consultants includes contributions from numerous small factors and writers in addition to the author. Read about their experience from the trenches...what marketing methods work best, which are a waste of time and money...and decide which will work for you! Learn and profit from the experiences of those who have been there and are successfully bringing in business!

Both are available from www.DashPointPublishing.com.

Glossary

Terms in the Definition column that are capitalized and in bold print are included in this Glossary.

Term	*Definition*
Accounts Payable	Amounts owed to other companies for goods and services.
Accounts Receivable	Amounts owed by other companies for goods and services.
Advance	A percentage of an invoice paid to a client by a factor upon sale of the invoice by the client.
Aging Report	A summary of a client's **Accounts Receivable**, broken down by customer and/or length of time the receivables have been outstanding.
Assets	Anything of commercial or exchange value a business, institution or individual owns. Assets include cash, property, and **Accounts Receivable**.
Assignment	Term used when **Accounts Receivable** are factored. The **Client**'s right to the accounts is sold, or assigned, to a Factor.
Bad Debt	Unpaid receivables which have been written off as uncollectable.
Balance Sheet	A financial report which lists a company's **Assets**, **Liabilities**, and the difference (shown as equity), on a given date.
Bank Wire	A means of electronically sending money from one bank account to another.

Break-Even Point	The level at which a business' total costs equal total revenue.
Broker	An individual or business who, for a fee, matches a company seeking factoring services with a **Factor** appropriate for that company's needs.
Cardinal Rule of Money	"Don't risk more than you can afford to lose" on a given transaction, **Client**, or **Customer**.
Cash Flow	The difference between cash received and cash paid out.
Client	A company who factors its **Accounts Receivable**.
Co-Factoring	A process by which two or more **Factors** combine their resources to provide funds and/or services, and share in **Discounts** which result. Also called **Participation**.
Concentration	The portion of a **Factor**'s total factoring funds vested in a single **Client** or **Customer**.
Credit Report	A report obtained from a commercial credit agency which lists the payment history, debts, public records, and credit risk of a company or individual.
Customer	The company who has received products or services from a **Client** and will pay the resulting **Invoice**(s). Referred to by some factors as the **Debtor**.
DBA	Abbreviation of "Doing Business As."
Debtor	The company who has received products or services from a **Client** and will pay the resulting **Invoice**(s). Referred to by some factors as the **Customer**.

Discount	The amount paid by the **Client** to the **Factor** for the factor's services; it is calculated by subtracting the total amount **Advance**d and **Rebate**d by the **Factor** from the face value of the **Invoice**.
Discount Schedule	A document that shows the **Discount** paid to the **Factor** based on the length of time a **Customer** takes to pay an **Invoice**.
Due Diligence	Information gathered by a **Factor** to determine whether or not to accept a **Client** and/or **Customer**. Also referred to as **Underwriting**.
Factor	A company or individual who purchases **Accounts Receivable** from a **Client** at a **Discount** from the face value of the **Receivables**.
Factoring	The sale of **Accounts Receiva**ble at a **Discount** to a **Factor**.
Fees	Amounts charged by a **Factor** for: a) **Application** and **Due Diligence** processing and/or b) funds transfer costs such as **Bank Wires** and overnight delivery.
Financial Statements	Reports, which may be requested or required as part of a **Factor**'s **Due Diligence**. The most commonly requested are a **Profit & Loss Statement** (P&L, also called **Income Statement**), a **Balance Sheet** and a business owner's personal **Net Worth Statement**.
Fixed Costs	Expenses which do not vary with the volume of one's business.

Invoice	A document from a company to a **Customer** that states the amount owed by a **Customer** for goods or services rendered by the company.
Liabilities	Claims on the **Assets** of a company or individual, excluding the owner's equity. Liabilities include **Accounts Payable**, other debts, taxes owed, etc.
Limit	The maximum amount that will be **Advanced** by a **Factor** to a **Client** for all **Customers** or for a specific **Customer**.
Lien	A legal claim against property or other assets, submitted to state and/or county authorities. **Factors** commonly file a **Lien (UCC-1)** against a **Client**'s **Assets** to secure against possible loss.
Loan	A sum of money provided to an individual or company that is to be repaid with interest. **Factoring** is not a Loan.
Net Worth Statement	The list of an individual's **Assets**, **Liabilities**, and the difference between them.
Non-notification	Term used when a **Customer** is intentionally not made aware that a **Client** is **Factoring** their **Invoices.**
Nonrecourse Factoring	If a **Customer** does not pay the **Factor** within a specific period of time, the **Client** is not responsible for repaying the **Factor** the **Advance** and **Discount** (provided the invoice is not disputed).
Notice of Assignment	A document given to a **Customer** stating a **Client**'s invoices have been factored and that payment should be made to the **Factor**.

Notification	The term used when a **Customer** is made aware that a **Client** is **Factoring**.
Operating Profit	The amount of income generated in excess of **Fixed Costs** plus **Variable Costs**.
Overhead	The costs of a business that do not include cost of goods sold; sometimes called indirect costs and expenses.
Participation	A process by which two or more **Factors** combine their resources to provide funds and/or services, and share in **Discounts** which result. Also called **Co-Factoring**.
Personal Guaranty	A contractual agreement between a **Factor** and business owner or corporation executive in which the owner or executive assumes personal responsibility and liability for the obligations of the business to the **Factor**.
Profit and Loss Statement	A **Financial Statement** that shows the income, expenses, and net profit or net loss for a given period of time (usually monthly, quarterly, and yearly).
Purchase Order	A document itemizing an order for goods or services from a **Customer** that includes items desired and prices.
Purchase Order Funding	A means of financing by which a **Factor** or other funding source **Advances** cash for a **Purchase Order**.
Quantity Discounts	A price reduction received by companies when they purchase larger amounts of a product.

Rebate	The balance of the amount paid for an **Invoice** minus the **Advance** plus **Discount**, which is paid by a **Factor** to a **Client** after receiving payment from a **Customer**. Its formula: Rebate = Invoice Amount Paid – (Advance + Discount).
Recourse Factoring	If a **Customer** does not pay the **Factor** within a specific period of time, the **Client** is responsible for repaying the **Factor** the **Advance** and **Discount**.
Reserve	The **Invoice** amount minus the **Advance** plus the **Discount**, which a **Factor** holds until a **Rebate** is due.
Schedule of Accounts	A document provided by a **Factor** that lists all **Invoice**s factored at a given time by a **Client**. It includes at least the **Customer**, **Invoice** number, **Invoice** amount, **Invoice** date, and signature of the **Client** with a declaration of **Assignment** to the **Factor**.
Spot Factoring	The process of **Factoring** one or very few invoices on a one-time or rare basis.
UCC-1	Abbreviated term for **Uniform Commercial Code**. A document filed with the Secretary of State and/or County Recording Clerk in which the Client's property being secured is located. With factoring, this filing evidences and perfects a factor's security interest in a **Client**'s personal property, especially **Accounts Receivable**.

UCC-3	Abbreviated term for **Uniform Commercial Code.** A document filed with the Secretary of State and/or County Recording Clerk to declare a change in a **UCC-1** previously filed, such as termination of security interest or another change.
Underwriting	Information gathered by a **Factor** to determine whether or not to accept a **Client** and/or **Customer**. Also referred to as **Due Diligence**.
Uniform Commercial Code	A law which regulates the transfer of personal property.
Usury	Laws (which vary from state to state) that regulate the amount of interest which can be charged to a borrower.
Variable Costs	Expenses which vary with the volume of business.
Venture Capital	Funds invested in a business usually considered high-risk. Investment is made by individuals, companies, or institutions, and commonly results in the investors owning a portion of the business.
Verification	The procedure by which a **Factor** confirms the validity of **Assigned Invoices** from a **Client**. Ordinarily, a **Factor** will determine the product has been rendered to the satisfaction of the **Customer**, the **Customer** intends to pay, and payment will be made to the Factor.
Volume, Monthly	The total amount of **Invoices** factored by a **Client** during a month's time.

Index

Who will benefit from this book?
Readers say...

"I absolutely recommend this book
- To new brokers
- To experienced brokers
- To existing brokers who wish to become small factors
- As a text in business schools for students of finance
- To the general business public wanting to know more about the 'mysteries' of factoring."

Joseph Leight – Santa Cruz, California

"Factoring Case Studies should be read by anyone who deals with money in their business, job, or life. Everyone else can ignore it."

Michael J. Minicucci – New Hope, Minnesota

"Any and all persons either already working as factors, thinking about becoming a factor, curious about what a factor is and does, and anyone interested in becoming a factoring broker, client or customer."

Ed Naglich – Etters, Pennsylvania

"Experienced, new, and aspiring small factors."

Michael C. Minchew – Ideal, Georgia

"Anyone currently involved in factoring or interested in learning about the business. It will definitely give a person reason to examine his own risk tolerance."

J.G. – New York, New York

"I recommend this book unequivocally to
- People considering factoring
- People who are currently factoring
- People who were factoring, got burned, and quit."

Virginia Sternberg – Mill Creek, Washington

"I definitely recommend this book to those who are currently or interested in becoming involved in the factoring business as a principal or broker."

Rob Columbus – Santa Fe, New Mexico

More readers' comments about his book...

"This book illustrates and drives home the material found in the first two books in the *Small Factor Series* by presenting real life factoring arrangements and explaining in the words of the factors themselves why some worked and why some didn't."
Michael C. Minchew – Ideal, Georgia

"This book cites examples of not only what to do but also more importantly, what not to do and the reasons why."
Ed Naglich – Etters, Pennsylvania

"Excellent! A ton of information is presented quickly in a very readable and understandable way. And the great icon system makes sure you don't miss any of the lessons you're being shown."
Michael J. Minicucci – New Hope, Minnesota

"Indispensable for would-be factors and factors currently in the business."
J.M. – College Station, Texas

"Anyone considering entering the factoring arena or those who are interested in researching factoring and its pros and cons should read this book."
Ken Earnhardt – Mt. Pleasant, South Carolina

"An extremely well-thought-out, well written and entertaining book.
Rob Columbus – Santa Fe, New Mexico

"This book is a 'must read' for anyone interested in becoming a factor, or for those curious about the balanced aspects of people and business in the field of factoring."
Joseph Leight – Santa Cruz, California

"Jeff Callender's books are a resource that you must have in your library. Use his books daily."

Reed Sawyer – *American Cash Flow Journal*®

DASH POINT PUBLISHING

ORDER FORM

Fax Orders: (253) 719-8132
Include this completed form.

Telephone Orders: (866)-676-0966 – Toll Free!

Web Site Orders: www.DashPointPublishing.com

Email Orders: info@DashPointPublishing.com

Postal Orders: Dash Point Publishing, Inc.
P.O. Box 25591
Federal Way, WA 98093-2591

Please send the following resources: _____

_____

_____

_____

_____

Please contact me regarding:
☐ Consulting ☐ Factoring my company's invoices
☐ Seminars ☐ Other: _____

Name _____

Address _____

City, State, Zip _____

Telephone _____

Email _____

Sales Tax: Please add 8.8% for products shipped to Washington state.

Payment:
☐ Visa ☐ MasterCard *Make checks to:*
☐ Discover ☐ AmEx ☐ Check Dash Point Publishing

Card # _____

Name on card _____ Exp. date _____